I Had a Father in Karratha

Annette Trevitt

Annette Trevitt is a short story writer and tertiary teacher. She grew up in small country towns in NSW. She lived in Sydney and London before moving to Melbourne to do a Graduate Diploma in Animation at VCA. Her short stories have been published in literary journals including *Salt, Griffith Review, Australian Best Stories*, Ireland's *Fish Anthology* and broadcast on the BBC and the ABC. For 15 years she taught short fiction, novel writing and screenwriting in professional writing and editing courses. She teaches academic communication skills to students entering university. She lives with her teenage son and their dog.

Annette Trevitt

I Had a Father in Karratha

UPSWELL

First published in Australia in 2023
by Upswell Publishing
Perth, Western Australia
upswellpublishing.com

Copyright © 2023 by Annette Trevitt

The moral right of the author has been asserted.

ISBN: 978-0-645-53693-5

A catalogue record for this
book is available from the
National Library of Australia

NATIONAL
LIBRARY
OF AUSTRALIA

Cover design by Chil3, Fremantle
Typeset in Foundry Origin by Lasertype

Upswell Publishing is assisted by the State of Western Australia
through its funding program for arts and culture.

Department of
**Local Government, Sport
and Cultural Industries**

GOVERNMENT OF
WESTERN AUSTRALIA

Contents

I had a father in Karratha, on the coast of the Pilbara in Australia's North West. The Tropic of Capricorn runs across the region, 297 kilometres to the south. Karratha lies between a ridge of red rocky hills and tidal salt plains that separate the town from the sea. In the daytime you feel you are pushed up against the sun; the early mornings and evenings are easier, often languid, but the nights are still warm.

Chapter 1
A fan was good enough

February 2016

I pulled over to the side of the road to take the call. Nerida, Marcus and I sat, three abreast, in our dad's ute, 45 degrees, no air-con, flies and, on the other end of my phone, the funeral director. We talked burial arrangements and then he asked if Dad was a big man.

'Well, I guess so,' I said. 'Yeah, he saw himself … yeah, in this town … in Karratha.'
Nerida leant forward and said, 'He means Dad's size.'
'What?'
Marcus looked at me and nodded.
'For the coffin.'

*

Our father, Richard John Trevitt, known as John, was six foot but not a large man.

In February 2016, Dad died unexpectedly in his house in the mining town of Karratha, 1,500 kms north of Perth, in

Western Australia. He was a 77-year-old retired roof plumber who had lived there for 42 years.

Dad was last seen on a Friday night at the Karratha Recreational Club (Rec Club) where, for years, he had gone six afternoons a week at four. The following Monday the club's manager noted his absence and rang one of Dad's friends to go around to his place. His ute was in the drive. His friend had to be the one to call the police when Dad didn't come to the door.

He was found on the carpet between his bed and the window. Dad had died in a heatwave of temperatures over 40 degrees. The air-conditioner in his house was broken. He bragged that he didn't need it – a fan was good enough – but maybe that night he did.

*

I took the call from Senior Sergeant Jack Russell at work, just after lunch. He wanted to know where I was. Two police officers were at my front door and the radio was on, yet no one was answering. I said, 'I'm at work in the city and I leave the radio on to deter robbers.'

I asked him what was going on. He said they needed to talk to residents about an incident on the street. I said I didn't know anything about an incident. That doesn't matter, he said, when would you be home. I said, 6 pm. We hung up. I picked up my notes to take to class.

Jack Russell. Jack. Jack Russell? And then it hit me. Jack fucking Russell.

'Oh my God,' I said to anyone within earshot. 'I just told a stranger who has the name of a dog breed I won't be home until six. What was I thinking? That gives them five hours to clear out the house. Jack Russell. Yeah, as if.'

I called the local police station.

'Hi, my name is Annette Trevitt. I just told a stranger who called himself Senior Sergeant Jack Russell that I won't be home for hours and now I'm freaking out ...'
'I'll get him for you.'

Later that evening at home, a friend called to see if my son and I wanted to go to her place for dinner. I said we couldn't as cops were coming over to discuss an incident that had happened in the street.

After a pause, she said, 'Is your dad ok?'

I had tried to call him a few days earlier and he hadn't answered. It was unlike him not to pick up or to return a call. I called his home phone. It rang out. I called his mobile. It went to voice mail. I left a message. Half an hour later, I tried again. It went to voice mail. Soon after, an email came through from my brother:

Ring me now Annette, please.

An hour after Marcus and I spoke, the police turned up at my place. When they left, I rang the Karratha police station and spoke to the young policewoman who found Dad. She didn't once let me feel the gruesomeness of what she must have seen. Without missing a beat, she said he looked peaceful. I didn't believe her but I appreciated her saying it.

The following night I taught a new class, firing on two cylinders. My mind couldn't settle and make connections I usually made easily. My thoughts, ideas and notes were all over the place. I showed clips of Jacques Tati to the students but they weren't interested. Dad had loved Tati but they weren't to know that. On the tram home, I surrendered to how I felt. Bloody sad.

> I marked assignments till
> midnight and only stopped
> when a blackout threw the
> suburb into darkness. I
> went to bed praying for an
> alien attack.

Phone calls to Karratha were endless. His drinking hole – the Rec Club – was having their wake for him Saturday night. I wished I could have been there.

On their Facebook page, they wrote:

> Vale – John Trevitt (aka Professor) – farewell old friend. It is with a heavy heart that we inform that our mate 'Professor' has passed away.

Dad was known as 'Professor' up there. He got the nickname in his 30s, not long after he had arrived in the Pilbara. He wasn't a professor but that didn't stop him loving being known as 'the Prof'.

> Dad's body has to have a
> post mortem. He flew to
> Perth today. Upsetting to
> think of him heading down
> there on his own.

Chapter 2
My father the hoarder

February 2016   **Karratha**

My brothers, Marcus and Justin, met in Sydney and flew together to Karratha. Mum and my stepfather, Tim, had driven down from southern New South Wales to Melbourne to stay with my 13-year-old son, Marlon.

The next day, an old friend drove Nerida and me to the airport. In the car I told him about a gold bullion Dad had bought in 1983 and hidden somewhere in his bedroom. We joked about who was going to get to the bullion first. We all knew it was hidden in his room but we weren't sure where. Under the carpet? In the lining of the wardrobe? Behind a dislodged brick in the feature wall? Marcus had seen it when he worked with Dad on roofs in the 1980s. The race to find it was on.

> On the plane about to leave
> ... got to tell you, Nerida has
> seen the gold bullion. Dad
> showed her when she was 14.
> He made her bite it. She
> knows where it's hidden in
> the room. Straight out of the

movie, *It's a mad, mad, mad,
mad world.*

Nerida said it's the size of
a thin brick. I'm thinking
like a block of chocolate.
Not Cadbury's. A thinner
European block.

Dad's house. Straight off an episode of *Hoarders.* My brothers
had to clear a path through the house. Marcus had cut away
some carpet where Dad's body had decomposed and under
the carpet, he found $500. Awful, truly awful for Marcus. He
thought that's what Dad was doing when he died – hiding the
money under the carpet. Plausible. Better than thinking he
was trying to get to the window to call for help.

A few of Dad's friends called in. Like us, they wondered if
he had died late Friday night or early Saturday morning. He
hadn't been seen after the Friday night at the Rec Club. Every
morning he drove to the newsagent to buy the paper for the
cryptic crossword. No one saw him do that on the weekend ...
or maybe someone said they saw him because someone always
says something like that.

In true detective fashion, I would have looked at the date on
the newspaper by his bed or on the chair but they had been
cleared. I watch too many detective shows. I sit in trains and
make up clues and red herrings for shows I've watched the
night before. I imagine going into work and my first sentence
being, 'Get this to forensics.'

We've started the huge process
of clearing his house. Dad's
friend arranged for a giant skip

to arrive today. First of many.
Forecast for the week 39–41
degrees. Feels like 50. No
air-con in the house. How did
he live in this?

*

The gold bullion wasn't where
Nerida remembered. Question:
who will get to it first?

Nerida's mother, Amanda, booked a flight to arrive three days
before Dad's funeral. I was glad that she wasn't going to see
how Dad had lived. Amanda had never been to the house. In
the late '70s and early '80s, when she was with Dad in Karratha,
they stayed in a string of caravans without air-conditioning.

Dad put all his earnings into property in Karratha. The house
was full of his belongings and of the stuff left behind when his
tenants skipped town. Something his tenants often did, especially after 2012, when mining construction was completed
and thousands of workers lost their jobs and the town went
bust. There was stuff everywhere in the house. No wonder
Dad had discouraged me from visiting him for the past five
years. There was nowhere to sit, let alone sleep. Stuff covered
all the horizontal surfaces, including the beds.

My siblings and I stayed in one of Dad's units – walking
distance from his house. We had five days together to empty
his house. We had to go through everything, especially the
papers, to find the bullion, the will and the title deeds for nine
properties.

Dad wasn't a consumer but he loved a bargain, a sale bin, a garage sale. As did his father. Grandpa would buy unlabelled tins from bargain bins and test the contents out on the family. Once Dad touched something, it gained an inherent value that meant he couldn't let go of it. It could be anything – a cracked mug, a cobweb, a broken chair, a petrol receipt, someone else's laundry basket, someone else's laundry, a shit-heap of a car, a house, an opinion, an idea – anything.

In a sea chest were some old baby photos of Dad. There was one from when he was 16 months old with his teddy that his mother got rid of when he turned two. Such a serious little boy.

Second skip arrived.

We had a system of throwing out. Nothing was to be double handled and everything went into one of three piles:
- to the op shop/front yard
- to take home
- to the skip

It worked surprisingly well. We all understood the size of the job and that we had limited time. There wasn't any of the shabby behaviour you hear about when someone dies and family members grab, steal or fight over items. That first night I had a thought that he might have put the will with the Public Trustee because please God don't make us try and find it in his house.

We filled two giant skips in quick succession. As we watched the second skip leave, one of my brothers was upset with the cavalier approach the rest of us took in throwing out Dad's stuff. He thought it disrespectful. We got it. For me, each time a skip left, it took away more evidence of Dad's pathology of not being able to let go of anything. Having said that, the finality of the skips leaving was sobering.

Not as sobering as finding out later that day, in the accountant's office, that Dad's properties were worth little and that he had an overdraft and a loan totalling $620,000. We had no idea. We thought he owned everything outright except, perhaps, for a small mortgage on his industrial yard.

> God, Dad lost his footing.

> No wonder he died. He would
> have been in free fall as he
> watched everything that he
> had worked for evaporate. So
> alone with it.

*

In 2015, in my kitchen, Dad told me that he had lost millions. I was aware that the mining bust meant property prices in the North West had plummeted – some properties across the region as low as a quarter of their value from a few years earlier.

'Sell, Dad,' I said.
'No, no, no, it's not as easy as that.'

What he hadn't told any of us was that he had an overdraft – a debt he couldn't service with the rental incomes – and that the bank owned two of his best properties.

Dad's properties were his savings, his super and his retirement fund. Looking back, I must have sounded flippant. Dismissive.

We found drawers full of brochures, flyers and letters from charities hounding Dad for money and from companies flogging lottery tickets. One folder was fatter than a city phone directory. In it, on each letter or sheet of paper, Dad had written an amount – $30, $40, $50. He gave thousands and was still writing cheques a month before his death. Fleeced.

Most weren't charities. I don't know what they were and, if I don't know, there was no way on God's earth that Dad did. Who knows where the money went? Although we had a fair idea where some of it had gone. His hall cupboard was full of synthetic towels, raffle tickets, soft toys, out-of-date calendars, shit pens, joke books, novelty ice-cube trays, useless plastic gimmicks and more envelopes stamped with:
'Anyone with the initials RJT is a winner.'
'A winner is about to open this envelope.'
'A star is born–we salute you.'

The Christmas before he died, Nerida and I were concerned about Dad's short-term memory. At times he seemed bewildered and unable to hold on to information. Each day he'd repeatedly ask what the plan was.

> We are on to the third skip
> and still we haven't found
> the will, half the deeds for
> his properties or the bullion.
> Maybe he sold the bullion
> or was it stolen? He hadn't
> mentioned it for a long time.

We had to plan the funeral. Dad's best friend, Bob, and Bob's wife, Nanette, found a funeral director 600 kilometres south for me to call. We drove around looking at churches and found ourselves outside the Karratha Anglican Community Church down the road from Dad's. The church is set back in a paddock of ghost gums and looks like an abandoned pizza joint from the '70s. A white cross set high on the roof, above the tree line, gives away that it's a church. The interior is clean, cool and welcoming. Perfect for a funeral.

Justin was upstairs when the funeral notice arrived in my inbox. He called out to ask what was going on. I emailed it to him. He roared with laughter.

> The funeral service was to be held at the Karratha Anglican Community Church in Bulgarra on the 5th of March, for the late Richard John ... Trevill.

Karratha was furnace hot. Nerida and I drove into the town's carpark, parked, ran an errand, got back in the car, drove across the carpark, parked, went to a nearby shop and got back to the car to drive to another spot in the carpark. Anything to avoid being outside. A pattern we repeated all week. Humidity was high – 85–90 per cent most days. If you walked around in it for too long, you went inside looking like you had been running for your life.

> Third skip full. Fourth skip on
> its way.

Amanda flew over from Melbourne. Nerida and I picked her up from the airport and took her to Dad's house. The house had been cleared of almost everything.

Amanda went with us from room to room. Her face kept changing shape. She went into the laundry and saw the shower – floor tiles were gone leaving bare concrete, everywhere wall tiles were missing, plaster had come away and exposed the pipes and the studs behind the taps. Limescale clogged the shower head. Amanda burst into tears.

On the dining room table, we had a huge pile of bills, invoices, letters, brochures and receipts to sort through. Amongst the petrol receipts and the invoices, I picked up a photo of myself as an eight-year-old girl holding my new sausage dog, Snoopy, that my maternal grandfather had bought for me when Dad left. On the back of the photo were the words:

I see you everywhere, my sweet Annabel.

'That's strange,' I said to Amanda, 'Dad called me Annabel for years but that's not his handwriting.'
'I remember that photo,' she said. 'It is.'
I looked at her.
'That's his handwriting?'
That's when I cried.

> The undertaker is picking
> Dad up from Perth and
> bringing him home.

The Anglican minister, Les, was relaxed and had a genuine love of music and theatre. I liked him. We told him we wanted the traditional Scottish folk song, 'With a Hundred Pipers'. He suggested the video of a Laurel and Hardy sketch playing 'With a Hundred Pipers', and then we'd cut to the serious version. I loved the idea but Les and I were the only ones who did.

> Getting ready for the funeral.
> Thirty-nine degrees and
> 88% humidity. Dad was so
> complicated. Judging by the
> state of his house and his
> finances, he was going under
> yet no one here had any idea.

The small church was full. We played a recording of a choir singing Bach's 'Jesu, Joy of Man's Desiring' as people entered. Some of Dad's friends had driven over a thousand kilometres to be there. The minister didn't know Dad but he set the tone and the pace beautifully. Dad's younger brother, Sim, from Queensland, didn't come to the funeral but chose the Bible reading: Corinthians 13 4–13 (Charity) from their school days.

Four of Dad's friends spoke of their time with him and what he meant to them. Marcus gave an eloquent, impromptu tribute. He spoke of his first morning in Karratha, when he walked to Dad's house, using his much-loved gum trees as a guide. Marcus talked of how he could count on them, like he could count on Dad. His sincere and generous words would have moved Dad. He would have loved being seen as a towering gum tree.

I spoke of Dad's history and the troubled times that took him to the Pilbara and of how my siblings and I are very much our father's children. Not just the full head of hair and the frown, the intensity and the shared sense of humour, but also the love of forensic observations, of story-telling, of pushing a gag and of the shared well-honed skill of mimicking one man – Dad.

I talked of Dad's love for Karratha. Justin called him Karratha's cultural attaché. Dad loved us kids but he loved Karratha just that little bit more. Dad loved lots of things – words, word play, cryptic crosswords, old Warner Bros cartoons, Calvin and Hobbes comics, Jacques Tati films, garlic prawns, family members getting on with each other, the colours of the Pilbara, his gum trees, the iron-ore trains, the Rec Club, his Bible, his friends, his roofs and singing.

Dad was a tenor with a beautiful warm tone. He had perfect pitch and often sang drunken renditions of Scottish ballads in pubs. In the Rec Club he was restricted to singing the first verse.

I spoke of how Dad was a different man outside of the Pilbara and how, after a few weeks away, he'd pine for Karratha. By the time every sentence had Karratha in it and when everyone he encountered – shopkeepers, railway workers, passengers on trams, people in restaurants or on the street – knew he came from Karratha, the hottest, driest and reddest place on earth, it was time for Dad to go home.

In the church after the first verse of 'With a Hundred Pipers', there was a pause. The minister walked to the pulpit and the singing rose again. The congregation laughed and shoulders dropped. Everyone knew that's exactly what Dad would have wanted to do – keep on singing.

We played Kris Kristofferson's song, 'Sunday Morning Coming Down'. The first time I heard the song, I thought Kristofferson was singing about Dad. He sang of a man walking around alone on a Sunday and how ordinary things – a church bell, a playground, the smell of something frying – took him back to what he had once had, and lost.

The coffin was carried out into the baking heat to Beethoven's 'Ode to Joy'. The funeral director, an out-of-towner from Carnarvon, led the procession down the Dampier Highway.

Nerida, Amanda and I followed the hearse in a borrowed car. I drove. Marcus and Justin joined the procession in Dad's ute. Ahead of us, the director flicked on the left blinker.

'Oh no,' I said. 'He thinks the Leisure Centre is the cemetery.'
The blinker stayed on.
'Shit. What do I do ... follow him or keep driving straight ahead? Quick, what do you reckon?'

We laughed. The hearse slowed down. As it was about to turn, its brake lights flickered and then the blinker went off. The hearse accelerated towards the cemetery but not before I had pictured the funeral procession doing a lap of the Leisure Centre's car park.

As we drew closer to the cemetery, we followed in silence.

The cemetery is the finest I have seen. Flat. Sparse. Rows of kooky graves in bright orange soil that turns a rich red in the evening. We placed Dad under the mid-afternoon shade of a very ordinary tree, close to other graves, in the middle of the 'dead centre' as he would have said. To the left was a dartboard in place of a cross. Next to it, a cross laced with strings of shells. Behind him, a guitar strapped to a cross. To the right, a child's grave enclosed in stones and a small wrought-iron fence that looked like a cot from the 19th century.

The funeral director was a straight shooter who, like the minister, was comfortable in his role. They both left us to ourselves but were there if needed. At the graveside, Marcus and I noticed the hearse was brand new but had a big ding in the side panel. On the highway from Carnarvon, the hearse, with Dad in it, had hit a kangaroo. Marcus laughed a lot. Of course something like that would happen if Dad was involved.

We had the wake at the Rec Club, where Dad had gone every afternoon in time for *Wheel of Fortune*. His stool at the bar was in front of a small TV screen. He'd watch the quiz show, shout out the answers he knew, socialise, drink pots of light beer – never schooners – and chip away at a cryptic crossword. That night the stool stood empty.

The other patrons made us feel welcome. Many spoke warmly of Dad. His unexpected death had shocked them too. The club was packed. Apart from the wake, it was a regular Saturday night.

My brothers played pool and Nerida and I poured coins into the jukebox till late. A pool player showed me a lot of attention. He was up-front, with beautiful eyes and heavyset arms. I liked his directness. I liked his interest. It had been a long time. Justin played a game of pool with him. Justin won and said to him, 'Now you can't have my sister.'

I was surprised my brother had noticed. I thought, well you can, but the thought was abstract. My family was there. It was a wake. We had just buried Dad.

The funeral director was returning to Carnarvon at six the next morning. I wanted to give him the cheque before he left. I arrived early and waited in the ute outside the motel. The sun was rising. Men in hi-vis drove past slowly, with their ute lights on. That's how everyone drove their work vehicles in the Pilbara – day and night. I thought of the hearse. I thought of Dad. He would have been one of those workers up before dawn to do a day's work before the heat set in.

Heading back to the unit, I saw a mother and young son walk across an oval. Just the two of them. No bag, ball, bat or bike.

The mother walked at her son's pace. Their shadows were as long and lonely as a cricket pitch.

Later that day, Amanda, Nerida and I flew back to Melbourne. We took with us seven cowbells, six silver matchboxes from World War II, the old family Bible, a handful of photos and a box of paperwork. I got off the plane in Melbourne without a clue about what was ahead of me as the executor of Dad's estate.

The first thing I had to do was find the original will.

Chapter 3
The runaway

Dad grew up in the small country town of Uralla, on the Northern Tablelands of New South Wales. His mother, Helen Lucy Sandilands, was from Scottish peerage, the Sandilands of Calder (Lords Torphichen) and his father, Richard Riley Trevitt, had left the Plymouth Brethren, a closed Christian community of austerity, in Sydney. My grandfather met my grandmother when he was a jackaroo on her parents' property.

Dad was the oldest of three. He completed the final year of high school when he had just turned 16. He wanted to be a vet but his father didn't want him in Sydney on his own at that age so Dad stayed in Uralla. In 1961, aged 22, he married my mother, Molly Juanita Blomfield, known as Juanita. By the time he was 28, they had built a house, had three kids and set up a piggery.

One night in 1971, Dad ran away. Mum only realised he was in deep financial strife after he had left, when she found bills and invoices rolled up in his sock drawer, along with a letter to say the house was to be repossessed.

Dad was bankrupt.

We had lost everything.

In the 1970s, especially in a small country town, to have a father desert you carried deep shame. It was never mentioned. I didn't meet another kid at school who had separated parents, or admitted to it, until high school, five years later.

I was seven when Dad left but I don't have any memories of living with him in the house. I was told I went with him on pig runs to sale yards. I remember the big, rattly Dodge but not the trips. My grandmother told me, when I was an adult, 'I used to worry about you, dear, and whether John (Dad) gave you water or not and fed you but you insisted on going.'

My mother said I insisted. She also said I cried every time I returned home. Hard to fathom why, as a seven-year-old girl, I had insisted on going to the stock yards. Knowing Dad, I would have been left alone for hours in the smelly, old, drafty truck. I loved my dolls so maybe I took them for company.

I was a watchful kid but, of course, that didn't mean I understood what I was watching or hearing. Maybe I had my suspicions that things weren't right. Maybe he said things to me. Maybe I went with Dad on the pig runs because I just wanted to be with him. I feel one reason I went with Dad was to make sure he came back.

For years I thought I had one memory of living with Dad. A time when I had gone to his chest of drawers looking for one of his hankies. The hankie drawer was too high to look in so I had to feel around. All I felt, and can still feel, was the dry plywood lining of an empty drawer. The memory wasn't of him. He had already gone. It was a memory of loss.

When Dad left Uralla, he hitchhiked to Sydney. He spent the first few nights in a park. He worked three jobs to pay off his debts. I don't know what he paid back. During the day he cleaned windows. At night he was a barman in the Mosman Hotel. After his bar shifts, he was the pub's cleaner.

The Uralla bank manager let Mum stay in the house for five months before we moved two hours down the New England Highway to my maternal grandparents' house in Quirindi on the North West Slopes of New South Wales. By the time we left Uralla, the debt collector had called in so often he considered Mum a close friend and was sad to see her leave.

In 1974, Dad went to the Pilbara. Any further west and Dad would have been treading water. He worked as a brickie's labourer in the port town of Dampier before moving up the road to Karratha. A town established in 1968 to provide a regional centre and accommodation for the workers of Hamersley Iron Mining Company.

Dad and a friend formed a roofing business. They didn't need to advertise. The iron-ore mining industry in the Pilbara was booming. Everything was under construction. The roofing duo put corrugated iron roofs on buildings in mining towns and port towns all through the North West – Dampier, Karratha, Wickham, Tom Price, Paraburdoo and Pannawonica, Newman, Onslow, Port Hedland and Marble Bar.

Hard to know if Dad's plan was to make quick money and come back. In the first few years, maybe he needed the distance between himself and the troubles back east but, as time went on, he fell in love with the Pilbara. He loved the huge scale of it. He loved the newness. He loved making money. He loved the opportunity to reinvent himself. He loved being up on a roof, high on the crest.

The region was transforming and Dad wanted to be a part of it.

In Quirindi, my grandparents built us a small house next to theirs. Mum worked at a school for kids with disabilities. She often looked after some of the kids after school and she looked after other kids when their parents went away. Mum was practical, pragmatic and resourceful. She held things together and got on with it.

In 1974, the year Dad went west, Mum met Tim Luckhurst, who lived in Quirindi's former 'Who'd A Thought It' Motel. He had recently separated from his wife and he also had three children. I remember thinking he was the most grown-up grown-up I had met. Maybe it was the British accent. Maybe it was his measured manner and neat clothes. Maybe it was the after-dinner outings when we accompanied Mum to see Tim at the motel and, as a treat, had banana splits with sprinkled peanuts and cream in a boat-shaped glass dish at a table with a white tablecloth.

A few years later, we moved with Tim to Camden, a town on the outskirts of Sydney. My brothers and I were still in primary school. Tim's three children lived an hour's drive north in Windsor with their mother. His youngest son, Adam, was in primary school and his two older kids, Simon and Fiona, were in their first years of high school.

The '70s – we all rode the first big wave of suburban divorces, second marriages, blended families, calling adults by their first names, experimental casseroles, weekend access visits and long, hot drives with eight in a car that comfortably sat five.

Every summer Dad drove 5,000 kilometres to see the three of us. The same distance from the west coast of Ireland across to the bottom of Turkey. Dad never had a plan. He would just turn up sometime in our school holidays. The visits were tough going, emotional, especially the departures.

I knew Dad loved us but it was hard to understand why, if he loved us, he still wanted to leave us.

I told everyone – kids and their parents – he was dead. Easier to say that than to say he was alive and for them to think he didn't want me, or worse still, for them to figure out why he didn't want me.

This made his Christmas visits conflicted and tense. I longed to see him but I didn't want anyone to know who he was. My greatest fear was that someone would catch me out in the lie.

I was in my mid-30s when I moved in with Lee, who would become my husband. We were laughing in the kitchen when he said, 'I just saw you as a little kid. I know what you would have been like as a little kid.'

'Really? What? What?'
I was eager to know. I hadn't a clue.
'Everything was on a hair trigger as you waited to see if he'd come back.'

The smile left my face. For many years, after Dad left Uralla, that's exactly what it had been like.

In 1979, Dad met Amanda Roe in the front bar of Karratha's 'The Walkabout' Hotel. He was 40 and she was 19.

In 1981, their daughter, Nerida, was born in Adelaide. Amanda took Nerida back to Karratha and the three moved into a share house with Hamersley Iron workers. Dad didn't stop going to the pub every day after work and staying for hours. In an isolated frontier town, the situation became unbearable for Amanda. She told Dad that she'd live anywhere in Australia with him but not Karratha. He loved her but said, 'I'm not leaving Karratha.'

Amanda and Nerida moved back to Adelaide and Dad set down deep roots in the west. In 1983, he bought his house in the suburb of Bulgarra. It was furnished with the same furniture we put in the four skips during the week before his funeral.

I met Amanda in St Kilda when she was 47 and I was 44. I met Nerida a lot earlier, during the summer holidays when she was seven and I was 24. I was living in Sydney and Dad had come over. We picked Nerida up from Sydney airport. She came off the plane, smiling.

Later that day she came up to me and said, 'What am I to you?' 'I am your sister', I said, and she hugged me hard around the waist.

Chapter 4
Sounded so easy in the will

March 2016   **Melbourne**

After Dad's funeral, my life took a new turn. Because I was the executor of the will, the paperwork was coming in. A barrage of invoices, documents and forms, applications and registrations and an endless stream of correspondence via emails, letters and phone calls to and from Western Australia.

I was flat, teary and overwhelmed.

For the first time I felt angry that Dad had left such a mess to clear up. I had to sort out shipping containers of stored junk, portables, a filthy, broken caravan he never used, and a small boat that hasn't seen the sea for decades – all in his industrial yard, a bank debt in the hundreds of thousands, his neglected house, rental properties (two houses, a duplex and two units) running at a loss, three, no, four missing title deeds and two small vacant blocks in New South Wales for which the deeds of one have never been registered.

I wish I could run away.

I was to pay the taxes and debts and then sell or transfer the properties and divide the estate four ways. Sounded so easy in the will.

The most pressing thing I had to do was the paperwork for Dad's accountant to finalise Dad's tax returns – one for 2015, and another for the months of 2016's tax year, before his death. After that, I had to gather the information needed to prepare for probate in Western Australia.

I had no idea what probate was except as a word used in lawyers' offices on TV shows. I had to google to find out it meant the courts had to establish Dad's will was valid and to certify that I was the appointed executor.

Once the Taxation Department assessed the tax returns, I could put in the application for the grant of probate. After probate was granted to me as executor, I could sell the Karratha properties and pay the debts.

I had searched again, in vain, through Dad's papers for the original will. I had a copy of the will so I contacted the two women who had witnessed Dad's signature. After a number of calls, including one to a woman in Karratha who had the same unusual name as a witness of the will, I found the lawyer who had helped Dad. She didn't work at the Pilbara Community Legal Services any more. She didn't know where Dad had put the original will but agreed I should try the state's Public Trustee. For the application to see if it was there, I needed Dad's death certificate so I had to wait.

> My brothers are still in
> Karratha, clearing and cleaning.

> Feel low. Last skip leaves Dad's
> house today.

The size of Dad's overdraft made little sense. He got it in 2007, when he purchased an industrial yard that he had been renting for some time. The mortgage was manageable yet by mid-2012, just before the mining boom went bust, it had doubled. By mid-2015, it had doubled again. It kept escalating. The rental incomes hadn't serviced the debt for a long time. By February 2016, when he died, the bank owned two properties – a duplex and a house he had built – and was cruising in to scoop up a third.

Dad was frugal. He didn't buy new furniture nor did he update or replace household goods. He didn't have holidays except for his annual trip over east to see the family. In the last 35 years, he had had one overseas trip to the UK with his brother, sister-in-law and one of my brothers, who was the designated driver. He was in his mid-60s when he bought his first brand-new car – a Ford Fairmont with 'plush grey seats'. He had next to no super and some shares he had bought over twenty years earlier. Almost all his income went into his investment properties.

I had a portfolio of seven Karratha properties to maintain until I could sell them. I have always rented and lived within my means so the world of property, mortgages, insurances, bank loans and debts, was unfamiliar. All the properties, except for one, had become money pits.

I had my work cut out for me sorting out Dad's affairs. At the time of his death, I was a part-time TAFE teacher in two locations in Melbourne and for an online college based in Sydney. I taught subjects, mostly fiction and screenwriting, in professional writing and editing programmes. Combined, it was a full workload. I prepared classes and marked online assignments until late most nights.

> Had little sleep. Head full of
> thoughts of Dad, his grave
> and the chaos of the estate.

*

> Had a class. Not up to it.
> Sick of pulling it together.
> It will take months to sort
> out this mess.

The invoice arrived for the four skips. We had moved five tonnes of stuff from Dad's house in a week. That's not including the ute loads my brothers took to the tip, the op shop and other people's houses.

Upsetting to think of the state he lived in. Upsetting to see the part of Dad's life that he hid from others and, in a way, from himself. Sad to think he didn't ask for help.

His friends knew house values had dropped, but no one, not even his best friend, knew the mess he was in.

> Had to leave yoga – too
> calm in there. Had no sleep.
> Overrun with adrenalin and
> thoughts of the mess. The
> junk and the neglect. Feel
> wild with the need to get
> things moving. Rang to

cancel Dad's home phone. I
said he had died and, wait
for it, they wanted payment
for a termination fee.

Chapter 5
Cryptic clues

March–April 2016   **Melbourne**

Dad had buried himself in alcohol and cryptic crosswords.
Both took him away from the realities he couldn't or didn't
want to face. My mother said in his piggery days he used to
read paperbacks or play his harmonica for hours when the
going got tough.

In Karratha, around four o'clock, Dad would head down to the
Rec Club or to a pub or someone else's house for a drink. He
never drank at home. He never drank alone. And then, after
being out on an average weeknight, he'd go home around
seven, lock the front door, close the heavy curtains, turn on
the TV for company, cook dinner, wash up and then, in a nest
of newspapers, sit in front of the TV and nut out cryptic clues
until it was time to trot off to bed, possibly taking with him a
folded-up, unfinished crossword.

I understand the appeal of the cryptic crossword – the solace
of unravelling and solving clues. I retreat into the occasional
sudoku, cryptic crossword or mind puzzle. I like the sense of
accomplishment, though short-lived, when everything else

feels insurmountable. However, they are never enough to distract me from what has to be done.

For me, the state of Dad's affairs was a torment. I had to get rid of the debts. The consequences of Dad's bankruptcy in the '70s shaped my dread around debt. I carried what he lost. Not the loss of the pig farm and the house but the emotional loss. He had said to me, once, on the phone, 'I lost my family ... I lost my light.'

Bankruptcy didn't do that; his decision to walk away that night did. His emotions had overwhelmed him and his first instinct was to run and hide.

> Sorry, can't make it tonight.
> Would love to but need to find
> someone to sign a Stat. Dec.
> so water to Dad's properties
> doesn't get cut off. Again, I
> had to argue against paying
> daily fines on overdue bills.
> Probate is months away. I will
> have to pay some estate bills
> and get reimbursed when we
> sell.
> Christ.

*

> Heading home from work. A
> woman in her 70s came out
> of the toilets and walked into
> the concourse, completely
> unperturbed she had been in
> a room full of urinals.

I woke early after fitful sleeps. Instantly wired. The sheer complexity of running the estate. I couldn't see how I could do it all on top of running our lives here. I just wanted to get the ball rolling and debts paid. The bills accumulated daily. The bank overdraft kept increasing even though Dad was dead. They went on charging fees and interest even though probate hadn't been granted for me to sell anything.

> Dad kept getting increases on his overdraft to pay the loan back with interest and lost it and more within months. Hard to work out what the fuck was going on.

*

> I'm sorry I can't come over. I've been on the phone all day with Dad's stuff and need to catch up with other errands.

*

> Was up until 12.45 am marking and hanging out washing. This morning I'm trying to finalise some paperwork for the accountant.

When trawling through Dad's papers for the accountant, I often came across Dad's handwriting. I loved his handwriting. Like his singing voice – strong, unadorned and sincere. I think the hardest thing to throw away after someone you love dies is something handwritten, even if it's a notebook of ideas and reminders or an ordinary shopping list.

A friend painted canvases of her late father's shopping lists using his handwriting – potatoes, carrots, tin stew, Weetabix, beans, chips, noodles, apple pie, cat's stuff. She showed us what satisfied her father. Like Dad and other men from that generation who lived alone, despite their complexities, they had simple needs.

One of the saddest images for me is an old man's back. The first time I saw Dad's back as old was when I lived in Sydney in my early 20s. He would have been in his 40s. Perhaps I saw it more as lonesome than old but tended to equate the two.

I don't remember Dad as young. Much of my time shared with young Dad carried too much unresolved emotional weight. Both of us always felt the intensity of him being a father who ran away. By the time that lifted, he was old. He grew old fast.

Last night I had barely an
hour's sleep as lay there
thinking of Dad and of all
the paperwork and for what?
Seven properties worth
as much as an ordinary
unrenovated suburban house
in outer Melbourne. I wonder
what his life would have been
like if he had been less proud
and asked for help. Had
listened. Been braver.

> It was all so out of control in
> the end but maybe it always
> was.

Dad's death certificate arrived. 'Cause unknown.' The coroner hadn't done the report yet. It seemed Dad had been married to Guanita, not Juanita. Change one letter and a lyrical word becomes almost ogrish.

I took the death certificate to get five certified copies at the post office. The postal worker showed such care and tenderness with the documents, I stood there crying. He didn't say a word. Reminded me of something Granny (Dad's mum) told me when the minister put his hand on her shoulder at Grandpa's funeral. She said, 'I thought, please no. No. Don't show kindness.'

Ten days later, I had Dad's original will. It was with the Public Trustee in Perth. Hard not to be pleasantly surprised by the sensibleness of Dad's decision to leave the will there and not in the house.

April

I found a small faded receipt wedged between the sheets of an old bank statement. Dad had sold the gold bullion in 1991 for $200 less than he bought it for in 1983.

> Overwhelmed. Too many
> assignments to mark. Steadily
> working through Dad's financial
> paperwork. Taking hours. Every
> time I type 'dad' in a text, the
> word is autocorrected to 'sad'.

*

Heading home. E.T. got on the
tram, He pulled out his phone.
E.T. phoned home.

*

Bought a chequered shirt at
an op shop down the street.
Can see now that it's on, the
chequers are better suited for
a tablecloth.

*

Had three days in Lorne in a
holiday house on the side of a
hill above the sea. Fantastic.
Back to another week of
unswept floors, half-hearted
dinners and unavoidable
paperwork.

*

Bureaucratic bottlenecks.

Another full day of phone calls
and emails to WA.
Another bill came through for
over a grand.
Another big Excel day on
Sunday entering all we need to
give Dad's accountant.

> Thank God Nerida can
> organise, file and make Excel
> spreadsheets.

In Year 10, my high school maths teacher had looked over my shoulder at a worked-out maths problem that had run over a few pages and said, 'Everything you do is a neat mess.' She was right.

I borrow other people's ways of organising and filing – I steal their sense of order.

Dad couldn't file or organise his files either. His paperwork ended up in neat piles in drawers and on horizontal surfaces across multiple rooms. I have no doubt he knew where everything was but his scrambled filing system, like mine, was only obvious to him.

Dad's notebooks were full of neat, hand-drawn lists, weekly calendars, columns of numbers, calculations and expenses yet they were just that – details. Dad never could see the big picture that encompassed the chaotic neatness. I saw his big picture and that made his notebooks of details harder to bear.

> Past midnight but I can't stop
> watching video clips from
> Richard Pryor's stand-up –
> *Live on the Sunset Strip.*
> *On Love. On Emotional*
> *Feelings. In the Jungle.*
> Watched *Penitentiary* for the
> 18th time.

'Why did you kill everybody in
the house?'
'Because they was home.'

I looked up a scene in
California Suite I saw 25 years
ago and found the scene. Just
as funny. Pryor's incredulous
face as he stares under the
bonnet at a blown gasket of a
hire car on the shoulder of a LA
highway.

Can't put myself to bed.

*

Sorry, I can't come over. I'll
tell you when I am free though
– between 2 am and 5 am
Tuesday night.

Jesus, talk about hectic. Long nights of working on stuff for
Dad's accountant. The real estate called to say some of Dad's
tenants had shot through. They left the house in shambles.
Work was needed to clean it. The overdraft was increasing.
The bank wasn't returning my calls. I was so over this and it
hadn't begun. How had Dad stood it? He couldn't have possibly thought he had a handle on it all. So much uncertainty and
confusion. Did he really believe he would recover doing what
he was doing?

Another late night. Finished
marking and couldn't sleep
and then couldn't get enough

of Richard Pryor's tiptoeing
buffaloes, talking cheetahs and
truck-driving buzzards.

Hey, you ever seen a turkey
buzzard?

*

On the train home. I've got
to put myself to bed earlier.
Working all day and night
is despairing when you feel
nothing else is going on.

At times, I panic that time is
precious and this isn't what I
want to be doing with it at all.
If only I could see an end to it.

I never considered the option of not doing it. What would
that look like? The Public Trustee take over and everything
is lost through a fire sale and administrative costs. I didn't
want history to repeat itself. I didn't want Dad to end up
bankrupt again. He had appointed me executor and I would
see it through.

*

I asked around to see if anyone knew of a lawyer. I wanted
one acquainted with property laws and with the granting of
probate in Western Australia. As Dad had kept his situation
secret in Karratha, I wanted a lawyer based in Perth. I'd gone
as far as I could without legal help.

Lost my temper with the
bank staff. Always someone
different. I have to explain the
situation over and over and ask
the same questions over and
over. They listen and then no
one, it seems, is allowed to say
anything or make a decision.

Can't wait for all this to be over
and I get to divide the $133
left between the four of us and
burn the paperwork.

*

Rampaging around the house.
Remy (our dog) is looking on.
His expression is something
between 'What's going on' and
'Anything I can do.'

*

Lost keys but had to race
to work. Hope I didn't drop
them in the drive and I come
home to nothing left but a
bowl of dog water and Dad's
paperwork.

*

Came home on the train,
texting, alongside everyone

else on their phones. We're all
muppets.

Forget phone calls to friends and family. Forget visits. Texts
were all I could do. They staved off the loneliness of having to
take on something so alien and huge on my own.

Texting on the train, along with
everyone else on their phones,
is as despairing as taking Remy
for a walk and seeing the
hideous blue light from a TV fill
a living room and then coming
home and putting my TV on.

*

Found keys under the pillow in
the dog's bed.

I need to sleep. I need to cry.

I had to compartmentalise grief.

In 2008, my husband, Lee, died. Four days after a diagnosis
of cancer. Marlon was five. The grief was all consuming. It
took years to feel back on steady ground and to adjust to it
being Marlon and me. To sort out Lee's affairs was minimal.
He didn't own property and nor did he have an interest in
amassing wealth.

Sorting out the complexity of Dad's estate overrode grief. I
had to get the chaos out of our lives.

When we cleared out Dad's house, I found an early Bruce Springsteen CD – most likely left by a former tenant. In the car, on the final stretch along the Dampier Highway to Karratha cemetery, following the hearse, Springsteen's song, 'Racing in the Streets' was on. After the funeral, I was unable to drive anywhere over there without playing the song over and over. I brought the CD home. Every time I got in the car, I put the song on. The soothing effect of the opening piano chords was instant. The song put me back on the road to the cemetery. It reminded me what I had to do and why. It reminded me of what mattered. When we followed the hearse into the cemetery, I wasn't thinking of anything but him, my father, up ahead, in the coffin on his way to be buried.

> Dropped Marlon at school
> and kept driving. I hadn't
> planned to. Crisp, sunny
> autumn morning. I drove
> around the bay. Nice wide
> curves. I needed to get away
> from all the work in my
> house and to clear my head.

Chapter 6
In the car with Dad

It's impossible to write about my father and not mention his, and, for that matter, the Trevitt family's, relationships to cars. Nothing was straightforward about any of it. This is shown in how we buy, run and get rid of cars.

The cars my family and I have owned:

1. the car that didn't start
2. the car that had no brakes
3. the car that leaked oil
4. the car with the busted radiator
5. the car with the broken accelerator
6. the car with the steering wheel that fell off
7. the car that couldn't be driven on a wet night as the headlights wouldn't work at the same time as the wipers or the blinkers
8. the car driven into the ground
9. the car driven until its repairs cost more than the car
10. the car that was a present to replace a dog
11. the car that housed huntsman spiders
12. the car with too few services
13. the car with flat, bald tyres
14. the car that sounded like a chaff-cutter

15. the car that crossed Sydney during peak hour in second gear
16. the car kept to keep another company
17. the car with collectable hub-caps
18. the car that moved a sheep across town
19. the car with side mirrors that bent down as if taking a bow
20. the car with a horn that went off whenever it pleased
21. the car used as a truck
22. the car that rusted to a shell in a paddock
23. the car bulldozed into a gully
24. the car bought with cash out of a shirt pocket
25. the car that caught fire under the backseat
26. the car with hammered dents of frustration
27. the car that took corners like a shopping trolley
28. the car that was a bargain
29. the car that was a lemon
30. the car that was stolen
31. the car that didn't have first gear
32. the car sale that sent a piston through my heart
33. the car kept for spare parts
34. the car that brought the family into the 21st century
35. the car that made the previous car look less of a shit-heap
36. the car that ended up straddling a verge

*

Years ago, Dad rang to tell me that he had bought his first brand-new car. For the first few moments, I thought he was talking about a woman.

'Oh, she's beautiful ... I've never had anything like it.'

We talked about the new car and then we talked about the cars we had owned.

'I love my latest car,' I said, 'But not as much as my old VWs.'

'Me either,' he said. 'I respect this car, it's reliable and smells great but I don't love it like my old one.'

'It's a different kind of love,' I said.

'It's not a personal love,' my father said. 'I think it's because the car isn't idiosyncratic. Can't latch on to its true nature. This one I could trade in. Just back it out and drive a new one in.'

The conversation ended when Dad and I had to hang up to go outside and give our respective cars a pat to appease our guilt.

*

Later that year, we talked on the phone about leaving our cars on the street. Dad had been invited to a friend's party on the other side of Karratha. He planned to drive the new car over and catch a cab back. He rang his friend to ask if he could park the car behind his friend's car in the driveway. At home Dad always parked his car in the carport behind his ute. His mate replied, 'No need to, John, you can park it on the other side of the street.'

Dad said he didn't say anything but he told me he thought, Oh no. It's not used to being on its own like that.

'I know exactly what you are saying,' I said. 'One night, in Sydney, I left my VW Beetle in Leichhardt after a party. The next day I walked over from Newtown to collect it. I turned a corner and there it was on the crest of a hill, alone and forlorn. I apologised and promised that I would never leave it like that again.'

Still hard not to see its bonnet as quivering.

*

It's possible our family's propensity to get attached to, and hang on to, old cars could be genetic down the Trevitt line and the Sandilands line. Out the front of Calder Castle in Scotland, our relative, Lord Torphichen, has parked eight dead vehicles: Land Rovers. The green ones.

*

To be inside a car with Dad was a different story.

When we were kids and he'd come over from the west, we often went for long interstate car trips. Always in summer and always in clapped-out cars with no air-con. Always in cars that never failed to break down and, with the flick of a switch, turn Dad into a ballistic hothead as he raged against his mechanical ineptness.

One summer, when I was 12, Dad took my brothers and me to New Zealand. For five weeks we covered the two islands – top to bottom – in a campervan that broke down at least twice.

We spent hours, days, weeks in that campervan, second-guessing Dad. He loved to quiz us and to test our powers of observation.

'That house we went past on a hill a mile back,' he'd ask, 'How many lights were on?'
'What did that last number plate add up to?
'The driver of the yellow car, four cars ago, what colour was his shirt?'

'Whose telephone number starts with that number plate?'
'How many cows were in the paddock on the left?'
'Think carefully ... why is the cemetery on this side of the hill?'
'How many times did the red man flash at the pedestrian crossing?'
'What did I see over there?'

We were dutiful kids. We never questioned the ridiculousness of the questions or understood that knowing the answers meant nothing. Instead, we tried to answer them and before long, we were at each other. We wanted to please Dad. We wanted to prove we were observant and smart. I don't remember relaxing and letting the landscape drift by. I scrutinised everything as a possible object that could come up in a question a few miles later. Even now I check out numberplates for familiar initials and number patterns, and know that the red man at crossings on average flashes thirteen times.

Looking back, I can see the questions were about Dad expecting us to read his mind and setting himself up as the smartest in the car but they also showed his focus – his attention to detail – was his way of coping. They settled his mind. It showed his discomfort with the situation he found himself in. On the road with his three kids, who he felt conflicted about leaving and who, for eleven months of the year, were growing up and changing without him. At times he must have felt at a terrible loss.

*

My brothers were in the car with Dad a lot more than I was. I missed some of the big Christmas drives. Dad never made plans. He'd just turn up some time around Christmas. One year I had booked into a week of horse trail rides on the outskirts of

Newcastle. When he heard that, he didn't ask me to change my mind, which I'm sure I would have done had he asked. Instead, as the boys got into the car, my father looked at me in a way that I'll never forget. Such sorrow. I was 13 and that night, I wet the bed. I was staying with family friends in Newcastle and slept in the same room as their two young sons. I blamed one of the sons – both were young enough to wet the bed but old enough to know they hadn't.

I locked them out in the front yard, where the mattress was drying in the sun on the upstairs balcony. I wanted the people in cars flying past on the highway to think that one of the boys playing outside had had the bed-wetting incident.

'Hey, which kid do you reckon wet that mattress?'

*

Tension in a car with Dad continued into our adulthood.

As he got older, he became more bewildered in unfamiliar surroundings. I used to take him for drives in Melbourne. I like driving and he liked being a passenger. It gave him an opportunity to look out and free-associate off street signs. Nothing could curb it.

'Peel Street. You didn't tell me we were in Tamworth. Remember Tamworth? Peel Street is the main street. Wait ... is that right?
'Davies Street. Bill Davies came from Kangaroo Island, would you believe. President of the Jockey Club. His wife, Cheryl, the club secretary.'
'Molly Street. You didn't tell me your mother lived here.'

'Stanley Street. Remember Stanley? Married your great aunt. You'd be hard pressed to find a man as dull-witted as Stanley.'
'Mordialloc. Now I've heard of that. Why have I heard of Mordialloc?'

On one trip we took Marlon to a hockey game on the outskirts of Melbourne. Dad was in full flight free-associating off street names, linking them to someone or to something random from his past when, up ahead, a huge road sign appeared on an overpass. Dad went silent. Marlon and I looked at each other through the rear-vision mirror and smiled as we drove under Ernst Wanke Road.

*

To be in a car, in the North West with Dad was different again. He didn't mind who was at the wheel – he relaxed.

We drove around Karratha. He loved driving up and down the streets where he had put on the roofs. Sometimes we'd leave a street confused over which, exactly, were his roofs.

'I put on that lid and that one ... wait, no. I tell a lie, not that one. That lid. Or was it that one?'
'Did that one and the lid behind the house over there ... wait a minute, which street we in?'

We drove out of town. He loved the huge blue skies, the pink hills, the burnt-red rocky outcrops, the muted grey-green vegetation. He loved the coastline, the estuaries and the rivers. He loved the mining construction, the Karratha Gas Plant at Port Dampier, the ore carriers, the iron-ore trains and road trains and the great stretches of highway. He loved the scale of everything up there.

Of course, a road sign and the occasional numberplate distracted him but mostly he wanted me to look out and see what he saw. He wanted to share what he loved.

*

In the car with Dad. It doesn't take much to ignite a memory from the enormous vault of memories of being a kid in the car with Dad. Recently I sent a video to Justin of a man mimicking the sound of a HQ Monaro going across the Nullarbor. He replied:

> I can see the HQ Monaro
> flying past us on that
> dreadful Christmas Eve
> spent on the Nullarbor's
> soft shoulder with Dad, his
> Valiant, no food, no cheer,
> no sleep, no future.

Chapter 7
Everything feels pressing

April–June 2016   **Melbourne**

In the months before Marcus and I returned to Karratha, the estate's paperwork and correspondence intensified. Things got tough. To keep it together took everything I had.

Apart from running a house, teaching, negotiating with the estate's creditors and combing through Dad's bank statements, cheque butts, invoices and receipts to retrieve and collate information for two outstanding tax returns, I became aware of the obstacles that Dad was up against as he tried to cope with his escalating overdraft.

He didn't stand a chance of climbing out of this quagmire on his own. The odds were stacked against him – the mining bust, the dramatic drop in property values, the bank's lending practices and lack of empathy and responsibility, the relentless onslaught of bills, the itinerant tenants, hefty tax bills, the high cost of living in the Pilbara, his age, his lack of technological knowledge, his pride and his bewilderment as to what to do.

Food, utilities, petrol, insurance and council rates in Karratha are costly. During the mining boom, the average weekly rent for an ordinary four-bedroom house was $1,500. This showed the high wages at the height of the boom. In 2012–2013, the town went bust. Mining companies had completed their massive projects, iron-ore prices slumped, businesses dependent on mining enterprises collapsed and workers were being laid off. New jobs didn't mirror the boom-time wages. Property prices fell. The average weekly rent dropped to $350, and lower again after 2014.

In 2012, the rollout of the Pilbara Underground Power Project (PUPP) to install an underground network to replace the overhead electricity infrastructure required Karratha's property owners to contribute 50 per cent of the costs. Costs that had blown out. Residents were sent out invoices for PUPP payments in the 2014/2015 financial year. The average cost was $3,000 a property. If you needed to pay in instalments, you incurred a 4.5 per cent interest charge. The estate was still paying off my father's instalments.

A friend had a friend who knew a lawyer in Perth. I contacted the lawyer, explained the situation and how I wanted to do a lot of the work to keep expenses down. He sounded experienced and reasonable, and became the estate's lawyer. He had to wait for the tax returns to be completed and for the Tax Department's assessments before he could help with the grant of probate.

> I just got seven redirected bills
> for the estate I have to sort
> out. Sorry, I'll have to visit you
> another time.

*

> Leaving in a minute. Be there
> soon. Already nine calls to
> WA, to real estate agents,
> accountant, utility companies
> and the bank. Can't find my
> life in this.

May

> I'm at the oval's gate for one
> of Marlon's footy games, in
> a fluoro orange hi-vis vest,
> waiting to escort the umpires
> out onto the footy ground.

> Oh, the umpires are already
> out there in the middle.

I love autumn mornings at Melbourne's footy grounds. Cold, crisp and sunny. And across the oval, past the players and goal posts, in the distance, trees are changing colour.

More credit facility fees appeared in Dad's overdraft. Apparently not all banks continue to charge these fees when a customer dies. I asked. Mine didn't. I would steel myself to call the bank and then get off the phone in a shitty mood. I was yet to talk to anyone at Dad's bank who understood what I had to deal with. Impossible to sleep feeling like that. No one had a clear answer about the fees, about anything. That, on top of an interest rate of 7 per cent. Every call to the bank felt like I was trying to turn a rhino around singlehandedly.

> My house was a write off.
> Cleaned it and washed the dog.

Feel better. Made a Campari to
celebrate and now can't find
the glass but did find out how
much there is in Dad's tab
account.
Sent a text to my siblings
offering the winnings as a
prize for whoever could get the
closest to it. Justin won with a
guess of $2.95. Twelve bucks.

*

Lists all over the house.
Everything feels pressing. At
times, heart thumpingly badly.

*

Letters threatening legal action
are arriving in my mailbox.
Computer generated but
unsettling. Takes some time to
get back on an even keel after
reading one.

The para-accountant, C, at Dad's accountancy firm was clear,
meticulous and easy to work with. We appreciated each
other's deduction skills and prompt answers.

We had email exchanges most days. She sent through many
queries ranging from wanting details of a sale of shares and
their purchase price, of unexplained payments, if the blinds
for a property in 2015 were replacement ones (like for like)
or new additions, which electricity payment was for which

property, breakdowns of the land tax for the properties and of the underground power payments, and so on.

This information took hours, especially as I had to decipher what some of the queries meant: 'Have XXX Limited issued an in-specie distribution advice – if so, we will need a copy, as it will show details of fully franked dividend and/or capital return.'

Hi Annette,

C here. Ok – back to the drawing board, and detective work. John's receipt book shows no detail; and the bank statement shows deposit. The advice that it was from that company, is as per the answers Nerida put together on the first spreadsheet you sent ...

*

Hi C,

The blinds were for the two flats in the duplex in Bulgarra. They were a new addition. (I remember Dad talking about getting new vertical blinds for all his places.)

*

Hi C,

The cash book where Dad entered the cheque details is confusing. In Dad's cheque books he always wrote what the cheque was for on the back of the previous stub, rather than the back of the actual cheque stub. Looking at his deposit book, it's hard to say if he did that or not.

So maybe the $1,746.45 isn't XXX at all. Maybe the XXX one is $35.35 – 7/10/14 (Hard to read actual numbers under the stamp.) If that's the case, then the $1,746.45 hasn't any reference information next to it. Does $35.35 sound right for a dividend from XXX?

Hi Annette,

Yes. Success – in one aspect. Yes, $35.35 IS a dividend, as is a later deposit of $34.35. So, the Annual Statement has been invaluable. Now, what on earth do we do about the $1,746.45? You could try phoning the bank ...

*

Dad was always short for repayments on his overdraft but that didn't stop him from trying. In January 2015, he got another loan for nearly $40,000. The overdraft continued to climb. In August 2015, Dad sold most of his Telstra shares to put into it. The overdraft had been at its maximum limit and was incurring interest of 11.16 per cent.

June

Hi C,

I was going through Dad's transactions in the overdraft since he deposited the $137,000 from selling 95% of his Telstra shares in August, 2015. It's astonishing how much has gone out. In February 2016, a week after he died, and seven months after he made the deposit, the overdraft had increased $90,000.

The money had gone into the running costs of hanging on to the rental properties and of servicing the overdraft that was only heading in one direction and had been for years.

> What was Dad thinking? Hang
> in there and weather it?

What went through the minds of the bank staff to keep lending tens of thousands when they knew the rental incomes were NEVER going to cover the outgoings and service the debt? Why did they let him? Why did they let him think he had options?

How did they not see a worried retiree, in his late 70s, who didn't use a computer and could barely operate his mobile phone, was in deep distress?

> Tempted to send the bank the
> meaning of the word, 'distress',
> so they can fucking well
> understand when someone is
> in it.

distress ... *noun* **1** mental or emotional pain. **2** financial difficulty; hardship. **3** great danger; peril • *a ship in distress*. (ETYMOLOGY): 13c as *destresse*: from French *destresse*.[1]

> Would they have signed off on
> the loans had the borrower
> been their elderly father?

*

---

1 Chambers. (1999) Distress. In *Chambers 21st century dictionary*. (p. 387)

Today I spoke to two share
brokers, a bank accountant
and then Telstra (they keep
sending bills even though I
took a medical confirmation
when Dad had died to the
Karratha Telstra shop). I
apologised for my curtness
and the girl on the phone
said in a soft, unfamiliar
accent, 'Madam, you are
very composed, I would be
screaming.' And then back
to the accountant and onto
online assignment marking.

Hard to picture Dad walking past the tellers and down the back of the bank in an attempt to sort out the overdraft and not feel his lonely struggle physically. I still listened to 'Racing in the Streets' every time I was in the car. The opening bars put me back in the funeral procession and reminded me all this was happening because someone had died and possibly died because of it.

Chapter 8
You've got no idea

Late June 2016   Melbourne

The preparation of Dad's tax returns and all the scrutinising of Dad's cheque butts led me to see a substantial amount of money going out but I didn't know where.

Hi C,

> Trying to make sense of one of Dad's cheques for $2,778. He put City of Karratha on the butt; that doesn't make sense. Rates aren't paid at that time of the year. I'll have to call you later.

> Took Remy for a long walk
> to St Kilda via cobbled back
> lanes. I needed to get away
> from paperwork. Melbourne's
> bluestone. One of the first
> things I noticed when I
> moved here – the bluestone
> laneways and gutters.

Hi C,

In the previous email, I said I couldn't find what the Cheque 335014 – City of Karratha was for. Well, I found it and it's not City of Karratha. I went back through the transactions of the overdraft. It's the bank's landlord insurance for two houses and the duplex. $2,778. That sounds a lot when they are worth so little?

I double-checked the transactions to see if the insurance was quarterly.

This, you won't believe:
That amount for the
landlord insurance for
the three properties is
m o n t h l y.

One house's insurance premium was $1,242 a month. The house was an ordinary four-bedroom Pilbara corrugated iron house. (The rent was $1,600 a month.) How was that possible? Did insurance brokers continue to get an annual commission – was that how it worked?

Do insurance companies just
make up a figure and see what
they can get away with?

I called the bank about Dad's landlord insurance to find what was going on. In the 88-minute call I managed to have the premiums cut by nearly $15,000 a year.

For the house with the insurance premium of $1,242 a month, the bank valued the house at $648,000. The house hadn't been worth anything like that for years and would cost nowhere near that amount to replace it. People I knew up there pay about $3,000 a year for home insurance. No one could make sense of what Dad was charged.

The woman at the bank went silent on the phone when we got to the policy on that house.

'I don't want to tell you how much,' she said.

Dad had never made a claim on any of his policies. At the end of the conversation, I was asked to rate the service. I said 'yes' as the woman was helpful. An automated voice came on. I was asked for a number between 0–10 to rate the service. I pressed 10.

Did she know her subject? I pressed another 10.

Would I recommend the company to friends from 0–10?

I pressed 0.

After a pause, I was told 0 was invalid. The automated voice asked again. I was sure it wasn't but pressed 1, in case I had misheard the rating range. There was another pause. Then the automated voice said, 'Thank you' in what I'm sure was an indignant tone.

I contacted the Complaints Department.

*

I knew some banks have a reputation for preying on the elderly but I also put in a formal complaint about upping a 76-year-old retiree's credit limit on an overdraft when it was clear his rental incomes would never cover it. The lending showed there seemed to be no qualms in watching him lose so much. No qualms fleecing him.

The Karratha accountant lodged the two tax returns. As soon as the tax assessments came through, I could send them to the lawyer.

> I have to go back to Karratha,
> soon. Impossible to know
> what's really going on and who
> to trust from thousands of
> miles away.

*

> Remy and I saw a mouse drop
> from the doggy door and run
> behind the fridge – so fast it
> was a blur. We stood in the hall
> doorway staring at the fridge.
> We heard something behind
> the fridge and took a step back
> in unison. I know winter is
> coming but I'm not placating
> that mouse. Not this time.

*

> Sorry, I can't visit today as
> I have assignments to mark
> and I need to answer emails
> from WA about water damage
> from a leak in a wall and about
> a flush button that's jammed
> and a leaking showerhead in

another place. On top of that,
another audit of my work CV
and evidence of professional
events I have attended for
work. Of which there are none.
All in by tomorrow.

*

I rang the real estate agents
to ask them to evaluate the
houses. I wanted to honour
Dad in the sales. I didn't want
a fire sale but Dad did love a
bargain, himself.

*

How did Dad do this –
endless maintenance – broken
air-con, broken security door,
busted hot plate, leaking pipe.

The real estate agent contacted me. Tenants wanted the rent of
a three-bedroom '70s unit to be lowered from $250 to $200 a
week. If I did that, it cost us to have them in there. The strata
levy on the unit was $2,340 every four months. A big whack of
that – insurance.

Then the added costs of rates, payments for the installation
of underground power and of general maintenance. I said
no. What I didn't get was that it was already half my rent in
Melbourne and, while wages had dropped, those blokes easily
earned two to three times what I did.

The open staff kitchen at
work has been renamed Staff
Breakout and now has a lock
on the door. The new passcode
is apt: 1953. What, worried
a student will carry out the
microwave or grab a turkey roll
from the fridge.

Who wants to eat their lunch
behind a locked door in a room
without windows?

                    *

A couple got on the tram. As
they sat down opposite, I
glanced up. The woman
flinched. She saw me notice his
husband's toupee. She glanced
over to check if it had slipped.
All that happened in less than
a second. He's oblivious and
she's a ball of tension. She
and I smiled at each other. Her
smile was pained.

                    *

Zoom in on the little video I
sent. In my kitchen, ants are
running up and down the metal
curves of the dish drying rack.
But it looks like they are riding

a rollercoaster – having the
time of their lives.

I rang another insurance company for quotes on landlord insurance. They quoted $381 a month but more likely $250. Not $1,242 a fucking month. I wanted to go to the financial ombudsman.

After that call, I rang the bank insurance company to discuss why that particular house's landlord insurance was so high. In 2011, the policy was $250 a month, because Dad said the house was custom built.

He was the owner/builder. The house is a corrugated-tin, four-bedroom, single-storey suburban house. The question the insurance company representative said they ask is, 'Does it look different from any other house on the street?'

Hard not to hear Dad's answer.

'Different? Of course, it looks different. You've got no idea.'

He was as proud as Punch of the house he built. He took me through the house in 1984 when it was under construction. Consequently, the seemingly arbitrary question meant Dad was charged as if the place had Italian marble flooring, an infinity pool and turrets. You could not find a more ordinary house – open kitchen and living room down one end and four bedrooms down the other.

His reply, 'You've got no idea' cost him tens of thousands.

*

I put in another request for a refund dated back to the first policy and to acknowledge the house is an ordinary project house. Similar to every other corrugated iron house in town and across the Pilbara.

I wrote that the questions to decide the policy were misleading. I also asked how it went from $250 to $1,242 in five years when properties in the region had plummeted to a third, or even a fifth, of their value.

*

I cancelled the policies. I didn't have probate so I couldn't access the money in the overdraft anyway, and I sure wasn't going to cover them with my credit card. Nor was I going to cover the latest invoices that came in. Dad's estate owed over $8,000 for underground power (PUPP) to his industrial yard in the Light Industrial Area and overall, owed $23,000 for underground power.

> On the train. A woman is on
> the phone discussing how she
> wants to lose another ten kilos,
> a young couple across from me
> are arguing about the angle
> of the TV in their lounge room
> and where to store the vacuum
> cleaner. I wish my thoughts
> could be as ordinary as ones
> on rearranging furniture and
> cutting back on sugar.

*

Walked past a car with a little
fox terrier/Chihuahua cross
in the back. As the car pulled
away from the curb, the dog
stared out at me as if it was
being kidnapped.

The Perth lawyers got back to me weeks after I had sent Dad's
personal details and all the information of his assets and debts
required for probate. I replied:

Hello R,

Thank you for your email and for (the lawyer's) letter.
My brother and I arrive in Perth at 10.15am on Thursday the 30th of June so we'll meet you later that day.

I have checked your letter for probate. There are a few
typos:

point 2   My father was born in Uralla, not Uraia, New
           South Wales
point 4   He died in 619 Melak St, not Malak St
point 7.1 Dad was a divorcee, not a widower.

Today was a good day. I had
my first free day of not having
to do anything with the estate
of John Trevill who was born
in Uralia, married Guanita and
died a widower in Malak St ...
seriously how hard can it be to
get details on legal documents
right when someone has died.
I can't imagine how I would
have felt had this happened

when Lee died. Dad – I can see
the humour in it. Sadly – kind
of in keeping with an aspect of
him.

*

I'm outside work on the street,
walking behind two robed
Buddhist nuns. Shaved heads
and ears as translucent as
bat's wings. Is it ok to say I
feel better?

*

At home marking assignments.
On a student's story is the
smallest caterpillar I've ever
seen. Ink black. The size
somewhere between a Times
New Roman point 12 i and a
comma.
Yet you can see the distinctive
undulating movement – the
stretching and contracting.

The bank insurers sent an email justifying the monthly $1,242
for landlord insurance for the 'ordinary suburban house'. They
stated on further review, the premium of the policy was calculated correctly based on business rules. They argued that
the sum insured was decided by the Full Building Replacement details that Dad gave the insurance broker in 2011. They
also said that Dad got yearly reminders and didn't dispute
the policy.

I want to take it further. There
is no answer to why the
premium jumped from $250
to $1,242 in five years and is
up to five times more than any
other insurance quote.

Other company quoted
between $250 – $381 per
month for the same conditions.
As their spokesperson said,
'Where is bank insurer's duty
of care for its customers.'

Where is duty of care for
its customers apparent
anywhere?

Another quote from an insurance broker was $3,692 for a year.
The irony was the insurance premium for his other house in
the same suburb was half, yet, the house really did look different. As Justin said, it looked like Spanish donkey stables. Dad
had built it too. His first house. Another conventional house
disguised under big arches, dark timber eaves, window shut-
ters and a façade of big, white, cement-rendered swirls.

The cost of the bank insurance fell back on an ambiguous
distinction between custom-made and project home. I replied
to the insurance company's email that 'because my father
didn't question the outlandish landlord insurance' was not an
answer to my question as to why it was nearly a thousand a
month more than any other insurance company.

I received a reply. The insurers apologised for the delayed
update. They wrote that they wanted to acquaint me with

their process and to inform me that the cost of rebuilding the property varies and the rates are set by their National Product Team based on the agreement between the insurer and the insurance broker. They went on to tell me several factors affect the premium. The most 'impacting' was the risk assessment when it comes to adverse weather conditions. They wrote that they may be able to change the occupancy type of the policy dating back to the time of Dad's death and adjust the current premiums.

'Impacting' is such a shit word.

Surely, before giving Dad yet another loan, the bank would have seen the exorbitant insurance premiums the bank charged for his ordinary houses. They would have known the value of his properties, especially seeing as the bank owned two of them.

> Nothing seems to be moving
> even though I've been working
> around the clock.
>
> I may not be in the business
> world but it doesn't take long
> to get it. Follow the money and
> don't assume professionals
> conduct themselves
> professionally or ethically.
>
>   *
>
> I walked past a half-opened
> door at work and saw my
> manager in a room with
> other staff members. I smiled

and gave a small wave and
continued down the corridor
and into the office wondering
why he glared at me. Oh. Was
I supposed to be in there?

*

Had the thrill today of a
student turn up on the last day
of class, in a silver spacesuit.
Silver boots as well. Helmet at
home. Huge smile. Reckons
he got on the train and no one
saw him. Too busy browsing on
their phones. What a glorious
sight to have missed.

Classes for the semester
have ended. Downloading the
assignments I have to mark
when in WA. I can't wait for
something to be easy.

Marcus flew to Melbourne to come with me to meet the lawyer
in Perth, and to go on to Karratha to meet real estate agents
and set up the sales of Dad's properties, clean up some of the
places and meet with the accountant.

We are heading to Karratha
on the 30th June to the 10th
July. Would Marlon be able to
stay with you from the 30th
(Thursday) to Monday? He
can go to another friend's on

Monday (4th) to Wednesday
and then Mum can come on
Wednesday the 6th and stay on
for a few days after I return.

*

He loves holidays and will be
up for anything.

*

On the plane waiting to take
off. Marcus and I in the front
row of Jetstar. Exit seats.
Our seats are so close to the
captain in the cockpit we can
almost tap him on the shoulder.

The co-pilot got up and is
standing in line for the toilet.
How does that work? What ...
when we're in the air, the front
end of the plane shares the
toilet with the pilots?

Does this bear thinking about?

Chapter 9
Deadlines

Marcus and I landed in Perth. We received a thawing muffin and watery hot chocolate for our willingness to man the plane's exit door. I had spent the four hours reading and watching half the plane queue for the captain's toilet. Didn't seem right he didn't have his own. What if he was bursting or worse?

We made our way to the hotel on buses. I went for a long walk – beautiful evening breeze – and had a celebratory beer in a Northbridge pub while Marcus slept in the hotel. The beer was icy cold and delicious, so I ordered calamari and chips and had another. Barely made the distance back to the hotel.

Perth is a strange town. Nice light. Ideal weather. A clean, rich, shiny-showy town.

The next day, Marcus and I met the lawyer and liked him. From the country. Approachable. A happy rower who loved the water in the morning. He has a life outside his job.

Later that day, we flew to Karratha. The country was surprisingly green. Ideal temperature of low 20s. As we walked across the tarmac, an airport worker reprimanded me for taking photos of the airport's roof. It's the architecture of a style I love.

We stayed in Dad's house. Terrible state. No flooring, shit shower. Everything from the windows to the stove to the air-conditioning system was in disrepair and needed attention.

We met a couple of real estate agents and agreed on one. I needed a real estate agent to match my restlessness to keep things moving. I needed someone whose pace met mine. I needed prompt replies. I needed action. The distance between Melbourne and Karratha made that crucial. I felt sick letting down the other that we hadn't chosen. Like Dad, I found making these sorts of decisions difficult.

But time had become something new since managing Dad's estate. Apart from the sheer burden of it all, there was so much toing and froing in the dealings, and with that, so much waiting and uncertainty. Time had become something to push against.

I wrote a list of who I had to see during the week. Various council departments to extend deadlines for rates and other costs associated with the houses, the accountant, an insurance broker, a few creditors and the bank staff at Dad's branch. I also needed to get prices for some of the essential things I needed to buy for Dad's house – stove, flooring, toilets, air-conditioning units and shower. It was a long way off before we could get the house ready for sale but I wanted an idea of what to expect.

There wasn't any money to clean up and fix any of the places except for the bare minimum that I put into the estate. But I couldn't afford to, and didn't want to, throw money into these properties.

> Marcus is an incredible physical
> worker. On his own, he will
> be emptying two shipping
> containers of steel and
> discontinued roofing material
> and clearing away building
> junk from Dad's shed in the
> industrial yard into skips.

As well as ticking off things on the list, familiarising myself with what went on up there and getting acquainted with people I had been dealing with on the phone, I wanted a holiday. A reprieve. The estate's ongoing paperwork and the online marking made it impossible to relax at home.

I went for drives around Karratha in Dad's ute. Dawn and dusk were particularly spectacular as a golden haze softened the harsh landscape. I often visited the cemetery. Dad's grave is under a temporary wooden cross with a small plaque screwed on, just that bit crooked. It's the first thing you notice as you approach the grave.

I drove out to Hearson Cove on Burrup Peninsula for swims. The beach is made up of smoothed broken shells. At both ends of the cove are striking hills of red rocks. You can swim there at high tide and at low tide, walk for hundreds of metres on rippled mud flats before you reach the shoreline.

> Heading back after a swim.
> Perfect. Stopped on the side of

the road to watch an iron-ore
train I'd seen miles back, pass
along a ridge behind the new
industrial area. Buildings the
size of aircraft hangars on
huge blocks alongside rows of
giant cranes and bulldozers.
Not like the old industrial area
where Dad's yard is located.
Smaller blocks with smaller
sheds, shipping containers and
rubble. I drove away thinking
it's all just men's junk that
someday, someone will have
to clean up. I thought – that's
what I'm doing.
The iron-ore train took a full
five minutes to pass by.

*

At the Karratha lookout. Came
up to see the sun go down over
the sea and over the streets of
Bulgarra.

At the bottom of the lookout,
across the road, I can see
Marcus. He's on the roof of the
duplex – working on a patch
about the size of a single bed
– with a broom and a 750ml
spray bottle of multipurpose
Orange Power cleaner. I can
hear him scrubbing.

I need a beer. A beer, chips and
cool evening breeze after a hot
day.

A beer, fish n chips and garlic
prawns.

Plan on that for Marcus's
birthday, at Point Samson. An
oasis 50kms up the coast.

*

The town is empty. We're at
the old Walkabout pub for a
beer and chips. Cavernous. A
few old timers on stools at the
bar. Big screens on the walls
flashing different sports. Sound
on mute.
The town's gone to Marble
Bar, 400kms west, for the July
races and annual Undies Run.

*

The first time I liked the taste of beer was in 'The Walkabout'
Hotel. I was 21 and had come 'over west' to visit Dad. I hadn't
been before. I did the 5,570-kilometre trip overland. I caught a
train from Sydney to Adelaide, stayed with my aunt, and then
got a ride across the Nullarbor to Perth in a Holden station
wagon with a Dutchman, Fitz, and a Canadian farm boy,
Sandy. A dead ringer for Alfred E Neuman's grinning face on

the cover of *Mad* magazine. A face that completely gave away his personality.

Fitz had found Sandy at a loss in a Kings Cross hostel after he had crossed the world to be with an Australian girl who had been an exchange student in his home town. She only told him she had a boyfriend when he was due to fly to Brisbane from Sydney to see her. In the back of the station-wagon was an over-sized suitcase full of unopened presents for her.

The two boys were easy to be with. We decided to share the driving and try to get across the whole way in one go. Hours in, around dusk, on the dead straight Eyre Highway, a kangaroo leapt out of the darkness and crashed into the bonnet and hit the windscreen. We pulled over and got out. Shaking and shaken. The kangaroo was dead. We dragged it off the road and cleared away the broken glass and got back in, still shaky. The three of us sat along the bench seat of the Holden, sharing a blanket, and stared ahead at the lit-up road for hours until we found a motel. We faced insects, the cold night desert air and what felt like the very real possibility of another kangaroo actually flying right into the car.

After a few days in a Perth hostel, I got on a bus and, 25 hours later, arrived in the baking heat of Karratha. Dad was waiting. He took me straight to 'The Walkabout' to meet his friends. There I had the first of many ice-cold shandies – three-quarters VB and one quarter lemonade – and packets of chips, always plain Smiths crisps.

*

Day of meetings and calls –
the council, the accountant and

organising the places for sale.
Feels good to meet people and
to have things moving.

*

Marcus hangs his washing over
the line exactly like Dad. The
clothes thrown as if hooked
over the line. The hanging
washing gene is strong.

*

Thank God the Karratha tip is
free. Marcus has done many
tip runs. I've been on three
with him.

*

Cleaned one of units of the
duplex to sell. Took hours.

Shame the bank owns the
place as it's possibly the best
of Dad's properties.

I'm thankful that Dad stayed with the real estate agent to
rent his places, if the neglect of his own house was anything
to go by. The women who looked after Dad's properties were
approachable and practical. Dad was fond of them. He often
did the repairs but he listened to them if they thought the
repair needed a skilled tradesman.

I signed contracts for the sales to start as soon as probate was granted. The bank still hadn't got back to me. How many times did I hear myself say that? I went to Dad's branch to see if I could talk to anyone but the person who signed off on the loans was based in Port Hedland or Perth. The tellers just said Dad went there every Friday afternoon for years.

We drove out to a rocky gorge
on the Burrup Peninsula to see
the rock art. Some are so clear
– hunters, kangaroos, fish, bird
prints, crabs, turtles and their
eggs and I think there's one of
a Tasmanian tiger. Beautiful.

Then we came back to a pile
of junk mail addressed to Dad
jammed into his mailbox.

*

It's pouring with rain. I'm
waiting undercover in the
shopping centre as I had
parked the car at the far end of
the open carpark. Could be in
a shopping centre anywhere in
Australia.

*

Meeting an insurance broker
to get quotes on landlord
insurance. Marcus's on another
roof, clearing off leaves.

*

In carpark. Overtaking a line of
cockatoos walking in single file
on their way to the shopping
centre.

Out at the cemetery. The rain
has helped settle the soil over
Dad's grave.

Roebourne races cancelled. If
the race track is anything like
the soil here, the horses would
be knee deep in soft orange
mud as soon as they shot out
of the gates.

Still out here wandering around
the graves and chatting to Dad.
The plaque says, 'John Trevitt.'
Need to get one with his
correct name:
Richard John Trevitt
11.9.1938 ~ 22.2.2016
Father, roofer ... fool

The way Dad 'managed
everything' and the state he
left it in. The way he let pride
and passivity get in the way.

When we were over there for the funeral, my stepfather, Tim,
sent a text:

> Your mother is particularly
> pleased to hear it's (the
> grave's) in a nice shady spot.

Mum's pleasure is genuine. She has an exceptional under-standing of how the sun's movement affects a place. Any place. So to know Dad's grave was protected from a beating from the afternoon sun reassured her that he was ok.

For me, the four-month mark is one of the hardest after a death. The person should be home by now, from wherever it is they have been, or at least be on the other end of the phone.

We drove to Point Samson for Marcus's birthday. We arrived at the Samson Beach Tavern at three. The kitchen was closed until five, so we went elsewhere and had cake. Disappointing, as all of us went to the tavern with Dad whenever we came over. We always had fish and chips, beer and garlic prawns.

We stopped at an estuary on the way back. One of the most beautiful places I've been. When you look past the mangroves, out to the horizon, you can see rock outcrops aglow in the ocean. You can feel the untouched ancient-ness and richness of the place.

> The tide's heading out. It's so
> tempting to dive in but even
> standing on the edge of the
> rocks, staring into the clear
> deep pool, you feel you are
> being lured into a crocodile's
> hole.

Afterwards we drove through Wickham, past an iron-ore port and out to Port Walcott Yacht Club. A shack above a beach where turtles nest. Closed. On the way home we drove down a dirt road to get closer to the railway track to watch a kilometre-long iron-ore train pass by on its way to the coast. The shifting colours of the sky and hills and the scale of these iron-ore trains are things everyone should see. The place is magnetic.

When we were growing up,
'over west', 'over there', 'up
west', 'up there' was an alien
place. The place that pulled
Dad away from us. Dad being
buried here, his death, puts us
in this place for life.

*

Walked past a local footy game.
Asked the players on the
sideline if the game was over.
'Half time.'
'How you going?'
'Coming second,' said a player
as he pulled back hard on a
cigarette.
I walked on and saw the
scoreboard:
11-4-70 to 0-2-2.

*

In Rec Club. Marcus's birthday.
He's playing pool. I'm in the
beer garden about to hear how
to drive a manual truck from

a baby-faced 25 year old. His
dream is to drive a three-trailer
road train. And to be on the
cover of *Outback*. He comes
from a family of truck drivers
down south but no one in his
family has ever driven a truck
that size.

*

Now I have the image of an 18
Speed gearbox in my phone's
photos.

Back inside at the pool table I met 33-year-old J. I liked him
straight away. Not just his exceptional wit and candour; there
was something about his sensibility. He noticed things in a way
I loved things being noticed. He missed little. He was present
and playful. Before long I was talking mostly to him.

The baby-faced truck driver went home. Marcus played some
more pool and then left. I stayed on, putting my savings into
the finest jukebox I know of and talking to J.

I couldn't get enough of either. It was so rare to feel free. It
was something I hadn't felt for years. Nor was meeting
someone new and feeling the exquisite rush of our synapses
firing together.

Glorious brain crackle over a pool table. We were inseparable.
The place was crowded. Lively. Noisy. The local AFL team had
won and were celebrating. At one stage they surrounded the
pool tables and sang along to Daryl Braithwaite's 'The Horses'
putting their all into the chorus.

J played game after game and I put on song after song. If he went out for a cigarette, I went with him. He continued to play and together we watched everything going on around us. I remember little of what we talked about. I remember agreeing a pot of beer was better than a schooner and heaps better still than a thick-lipped jar. A blond mullet of a shy teenager who had come in for a night out with his grandmother triggered a lengthy conversation about having a rat's tail.

'... and who do you turn to, to confirm that the rat tail works?'

Five inseparable hours. What I do remember of that night was the falling away of my guard. For the first time in years, I had met someone new and didn't feel the need to entertain or to keep the show going for their sake or mine. We weren't trying to get to know each other or to find common ground. We didn't need to. I can count on one hand how often I have felt that kind of connection.

Only when the Rec Club closed, and we were parting, did I see he felt as I had. He was confused when I said goodbye but by then it was too late. My guard was back up. Self-consciousness had kicked in. I had let our age difference come into play and affect how I saw us.

> I'm leaving tomorrow. Lots got sorted in Karratha. Marcus is staying on to clear away Dad's stuff from the industrial block. Big job.

*

> I looked up names of colours to describe the shades of green

in the hummocks of grass
here. The two closest ones are
sage and asparagus – cooked
asparagus, not fresh.

On my last night in Karratha, I went out again. I saw N, who
had shown an interest at Dad's wake. He was closer to my age
than J. He apologised for his directness the last time we met.
Perhaps because it had been during Dad's wake but I assured
him it was fine. We had a short chat, and, before I knew it, I said
if he wanted, I could go home with him that night. This was
not my style. The bluntness hid the fact that I was as shocked
at my words as he was but I had had a week of thinking about
it and of working on my bravado. He smiled and went out the
back to his friends. Ten, fifteen minutes later, he came back in.
I was pouring other people's coins into the jukebox as he asked
if he had heard right. I said, 'Yes.' He smiled and went back
out. I hung around the jukebox, chewing ice from my vodka
and soda, smiling inanely and acting as though controlling the
music meant I was in control of the situation.

Later, as we left to walk to his place, I think he felt as I felt.
Unsure and overwhelmed. He was loud with his friends but
shy with me. I was far too sober. I told him it had been a long
time, too long. He said for him, too. He offered to hold my
hand. I regret my response of not accepting the kindness of
the gesture. Both of us had needed the reassurance.

It was still dark when I snuck back in through the bedroom
window of Dad's house, not to wake Marcus sleeping in the
living room. Felt like a teenager. A happy teenager.

*

Boarded the plane to Melbourne at 11:50 pm. I slept on and off on the flight home from Perth between two middle-aged men. One was an uptight, humourless professional who had the demeanour of an indulged schoolboy and the other was a big-wristed, warm-hearted bear. The bear slept soundly through the night. The uptight one watched episodes of *Auction Hunters* for the entire trip. Every time I opened my eyes, he was watching another auction. Landed at 5:15 am. As we taxied into Tullamarine, he woke the woman back in Perth who he had been messaging when we boarded to tell her he had landed – 3:15 am her time.

> May I recommend that you
> never catch the red eye.

Chapter 10
Bottlenecks

Late July–August 2016   **Melbourne**

Melbourne felt like a morgue after the Pilbara. Everything felt sedate, manicured and fenced in. Maybe it's my area. Every time a new place goes up, so does a high fence that blocks the garden and the entrance from being viewed from the street.

I came back to more of the same – teaching, marking assignments and dealing with paperwork for the estate, which had ramped up with the impending house sales. The days were full and the nights were low on sleep.

> Home, trapped between piles
> of paper for the estate and
> for TAFE. I thought peak
> paperwork happened a few
> years ago but I was wrong.
> Why the relentless obsession
> with 'updated' and 'new' forms.
> Imagine if everyone printed off
> all their hidden computer files.
> That would show the world the
> sheer madness.

The reason for that particular round of 'updated' and 'new' forms was the changing of one word. Somewhere it was decided that TAFE students were to be called 'learners'. I will never call a student a 'learner'. Verbally or on paper. Demeaning for everyone involved. I don't know a teacher who would.

Years ago, an experienced long-term TAFE teacher from another institution told me she resigned after she had gone to a meeting that had projected, on a big screen, a diagram of the institution's new structure. The CEO at the top and then layer upon layer of brick-sized boxes to show the different levels of management and along the bottom was a long thin line – a skirting board. Its title: 'Delivery'. A hierarchal structure of an educational institution that hadn't included the word 'teacher'.

> Tenants shot through from
> another of Dad's houses. The
> agent selling the house told
> me, after trying to get access
> to the house. That's when
> everyone found out.

> The tenants had dinner, got
> up, grabbed their bags, walked
> out the door, made their way
> to the airport and boarded a
> plane home to France. They
> left behind unpaid rent and
> bills, dirty plates on the table
> and pots and pans on the stove
> and in the sink.

>   *

As if they had jumped up
from the table to see what the
commotion was outside.

*

Until today I didn't grasp the
pressure I am under coping
with Dad's stuff and taking on
extra marking to cover bills. I
did the dumbest thing. I can
hardly bring myself to say it.

That morning, Marlon was at school and I was marking assignments and replying to the odd email here and there from
Western Australia when one of Lee's friends, who happened to
be in Europe, sent an email. He asked for a short-term loan of
$1,000 to put down a deposit on some land in the Philippines.
Urgent. I thought, this is weird. This is not like him to ask for
money? He'd never mentioned the Philippines but maybe he
wants to live overseas but closer to Australia? I thought, he
must be truly desperate to ask me. I emailed back. The frantic,
detached tone and poor grammar in the reply were unlike him
but again I thought, he's desperate and will lose the deal if I
don't help. Instructions came through on how and where to
transfer the money. I rang Western Union to understand the
process.

After nearly an hour of email exchanges and staying on the
phone to Western Union to ensure the details were right, I hit
the send button.

'Do you know the person you sent the money to?' asked the
operator.
'What? No. He's the lawyer of ... oh God, NO.'

Western Union stopped the transaction. I cried. Not because I had transferred money to a scamming stranger in the Philippines and was clearly not coping, but because I was alone and had no one to turn to when I got the email and say, 'Hey, listen to this ...'

There's a website called
foolproofliving.com
Big claim.

On one of Dad's last visits, I asked him not to leave a mess to clean up. He got upset, thinking I was anticipating his death. When I said that, I was thinking of his industrial yard and how would I ever be able to sort that out from Melbourne.

Years earlier, six weeks after Lee's death, Marlon and I flew over to visit Dad. We had booked the flights a few weeks before Lee died. He was to come with us.

Dad took us out to the industrial block, which was a junkyard. In a back corner, buried in knee-high rubble, discarded machinery and tools, was a filthy, broken, mouldy caravan Dad had picked up for a song. As we zigzagged towards it, Dad asked if Marlon (with me) wanted to spend a night in it. I laughed, assuming the offer was a joke. He looked at me and asked again. When, where, did he get the idea that we would want to spend a night in a neglected caravan, without electricity or water, in squalor, at the back of a junkyard in an industrial estate?

When we went up for Dad's funeral, I was relieved to see the yard. Apart from the huge shed, the portables, the shipping containers packed with roofing material and the caravan up the back, the young mechanic who ran his business there had cleaned up the grounds.

Someone told my brother
that Dad had sold him
the caravan but he hadn't
anywhere to park it.

Marcus, like Dad, liked to help people. He wanted to offer the
shed attached to Dad's duplex that the bank owned and was
soon to go on the market as a place to park the caravan.

I texted back 'no'. I can't let anything jeopardise the sale. He
said, it will show potential buyers how big the shed is. But I
knew it would never be picked up and I'd be left with the job
of getting rid of it.

So much to deal with up
there. I have to go back to
Karratha in the next school
holiday before it gets too
hot. Everything is falling into
a vortex. On a deeper level,
Dad was lonely up there
and that accounts for his
people-pleasing to so many
who would never have done
the same for him.

Fit in or fuck off.

What a mentality.

I felt we were cleaning up the aftermath of 40 years of Dad's
people-pleasing and problem-fixing. He had a 'mate' stay rent-
free in one of his houses for years. He knew the 'mate' would
never have done that for him. After eight years of mostly free
rent during a mining boom, I found a Statutory Declaration

that Dad had to sign to say his mate's final electricity bill at the house wasn't his bill.

At times Dad struggled to know if a friendship was genuine. If he did see a friend was taking advantage of him, he could never act to address the situation. The above situation upset him. He didn't like how he felt about it but he hated confrontation more. At times he got angry talking about it. He wanted people to 'come good' and do the right thing. Really, he was angry at his own lack of courage to deal with a contentious situation.

Initially he had let his mate stay in the house because he didn't want to chuck out an elderly near-blind parent who also lived there at the time. After she died, whenever Dad mentioned the place and one of us would say, 'Pass it to a real estate agent, Dad,' the reply was always, 'No. No. I have an idea.'

The family understood his 'ideas' and how they could drag on for years as just that, ideas.

I found a piece of paper in a clean-up where I had handwritten notes for an idea for a short story from years before. The character in the story had become aware of her family's different ways of coping when they felt they didn't fit in or belong. At the bottom of the page was the note, Ring Dad.

Marcus sent me a text to say he wanted to offer the strung-out ex-partner of the tenant of one of the units in the duplex the same back shed to stay in. I texted back, No way, we can't have potential buyers finding him there.

My brother was concerned. He wanted to help him and saw the offer as a solution but would the tenant want her ex-partner out the back? Would he really want to live in a tin shed behind where his young kids were living? That's a sad picture. Would he really want to explain to the young-gun real estate agent when he rolls up the roller door, alongside a potential buyer, why he was curled up in the dark on a cement shed floor in a tangle of his belongings?

I, too, find saying 'no' difficult although I know that other people's low points and their threshold for emotional turbulence and their ideas of possible solutions are not the same as mine. I'm at my most placating or people-pleasing when I feel out of place or uncomfortable in a tricky emotional situation or when I feel guilty for finding a person tedious, or for thinking too much has been asked of me. A lot of my family members, including myself, struggle to know we have the right to say no and to set boundaries.

Marcus sent me an email to ask me to stop talking about clearing up after men and their junk as this made him feel guilty. He then wrote a paragraph detailing all the stuff he has brought into Dad's house that we could use and would come in handy and save us a lot of money: fly screens, doors, tools, tiles and bed bases. I loved it. I got it. I went to bed, feeling good – loose and light from a hearty laugh.

> On the way to work, I got a letter stating Karratha city inspectors wanted to inspect the street where Dad's yard is and check buildings, the yard's safety and who's living there. We are screwed on all fronts. Dad has portables out there that would cost thousands for the estate to remove. This has to be a test.

Some tenants smashed a door. I had to make sure they paid for it. It seemed they thought they didn't have to. I was over work, over marking, over real estate chaos. A part of me would have loved to say, fuck it, let the Public Trustee take over. Of course, I never would but my God, it was arduous and at times lonely.

No wonder I wanted some uncomplicated attention when I was over there.

Springsteen's 'Racing in the Streets' was still on high rotation. I couldn't drive anywhere without playing it. It forced introspection. It tethered my thoughts. It reminded me of my love for Dad. The lyrics didn't really stick but ironically, they were about growing up and taking responsibility for someone you love.

> Marcus heads home from
> Karratha on Tuesday. He
> cleared out the shipping
> containers for the wreckers
> to take away. Back-
> breaking work.

*

> More bottlenecks

*

> *Background Briefing* is about
> Australian banks rorting the
> system including Dad's bank.
> Too much money, too many
> lap-dancing bars as meeting
> rooms.

How loutish are the traders in
their emails? Young unpleasant
white-collar tools.

*

Went for a walk down Elwood
canal. Dry. Some ducks
waddling around. In the
distance there were big shapes
strewn across the canal floor.
I got closer and saw they
weren't dumped TV sets but
boulders. They made less
sense than TV sets.

August

I lodged a complaint with the financial ombudsman about the
landlord insurance premiums.

Wild wind outside. Can feel it
coming in under the door.

*

In the middle of all this chaos
is my farm-boy father. A farm
boy with dreams who never
had his father's approval.

He wasn't alone.

*

On the way home, I saw a
Neil Diamond CD on an op
shop sale table out the front
and remembered a comment
I had read on a YouTube
video.
An American woman wrote
she had heard 'Sweet
Caroline' but never really
heard it. She had just left her
attorney's office. After three
years of hell, the termination
agreement with her
ex-husband had been signed.
It was over. She drove off and
the song came on the radio.
She was about to change
stations when suddenly she
was smiling for the first time
in a long time. She drove
down the freeway screaming
out the words. 'Holy crap,'
she wrote. 'The feeling was
unbelievable.'
I bought the CD.

See if I can hear what she
heard.

*

I rang Landgate in Perth
to find out how to find or
replace lost property deeds.
They have all the information

on properties in the west.
Helpful. I have pages of
notes. I can't do anything
until probate but I want to be
prepared.

*

I'd like to come over but can't.
Day is crammed with phone
calls and emails and forms to
fill. My second teaching job
takes up all my evenings. It
helps to pay for expenses
associated with Dad's
estate – marketing costs
and outstanding bills. Tens
of thousands so far. Sorry, I
can't come. Have fun.

*

One day I can lie under a tree
on the bank of an estuary.

Chapter 11
I can sell the houses

August 2016   Melbourne

Probate came through. I could sell the houses and then pay off the debts. I had to go back to Karratha to make sure the two properties were ready for sale. Trouble was, the biggest thing I had ever sold was a second-hand IKEA table on eBay. I had a garage sale once, made $30. Another time I joined a friend's garage sale and made seven dollars; three of that was from selling a toy cricket bat to a little kid in a fez.

Actually, I sold my VW Beetle for a few hundred. Nearly killed me. I felt the car had got me through my 20s. Took two hours before I let two boys buy it. To my dismay, they wanted to strip it and turn it into a dune buggy. Only sold it because when one boy said to the other, 'What the fuck is going on with her?' the other one replied, 'It's all right, mate, she loves her car.'

I took a hub-cap home on the tram. Cried all the way.

> Heading home after work. Just got a call from the real estate agent – he wants to drastically reduce the price of a property.

Already. I'll call him back when
the headache clears.

*

Drowning in paperwork and
although probate has come
through, I can't pay any
creditors as there's still no
money. Flights are thinning
out to get to Karratha. Can't
make a decision. I have to
go now because it's term
holidays and it's too hot
between October and March.
Truth is, I hate leaving
Marlon.

*

Booked. A friend offered to
be a sounding board. Head is
pounding. Done.

*

On my way to work, a bloke
has his lunch laid out on the
tram seat. I suspect he's
been here all morning. Colour
and movement outside. Quiet
and as warm as toast inside.
He's holding a sandwich in
his mouth as he sorts out
the contents of his pockets

on another seat. We're on
nodding terms.

*

Hi, would you be able to
look after Marlon on the
night of Friday the 4th? He
may have a hockey game
if they get through to the
finals. I'll get someone to
take him and drop him back
to you. I won't know till late
Friday night after this week's
semi-finals.

Two weeks in Karratha to
get everything done and
then two weeks here to get
everything back on track.
Wait, that's not a holiday.

*

2:10 pm. On hold to Tax
Department as need to get
a new TFN (tax file number)
for Dad's estate. Can't
leave house. 55 minutes
on the phone to the bank
being passed around from
one person to another, and
then cut off. One day I'll be
sipping a highball on a beach.
Isn't highball a great word.

3:18 pm. Still on phone
to the Tax Department for
another reason. Dad was
losing so much money
so fast, yet owes the Tax
Department $11,000. Never
stops. Leaving for Geelong
at five. Marlon's hockey
game. Head is pounding.

A kafuffle at hockey. Judy
forgot to set the clock for
the second half of the game.
Device was in the canteen. I
heard a woman say, 'You had
one job, Judy: one.'

Judy's in her late 60s. Soft
face. Floral apron. Puffy hands.
Crestfallen. Next to her, under
the counter, is a shelf. On
it – a half-eaten hotdog.

*

The estate is haemorrhaging
thousands through interest
and bank fees and here I am
counting coins for petrol.

*

My life is in a bureaucratic
maelstrom (never used that
word before). One thing

that's become apparent is
the higher your professional
position the greater the
possibility of incompetence.
Such little attention to detail.
Such little care.

*

Finding Dad's handwritten
notes amongst the estate's
papers – brings up a lot.

It only occurred to me when writing this that I was always
going to sort out Dad's affairs regardless of how and when
he died. He trusted me. He knew I was fair and saw things
through. He knew I was dogged.

During a trip over there in my 30s, at a party, I overheard Dad
talking to the host's wife, 'When the time comes,' he said. 'I'll
do what she says.'

I was shocked to hear Dad say that but looking back, it showed
he knew he always had me.

I woke thinking of all I need
to do in Karratha. Toilets,
shower, windows, locks,
flooring, stove, kitchen
cupboards, wardrobes, a
gutted bathroom. But I'm
getting ahead of myself.

*

It's hard to trust from
5,000kms away when you have
no connection with the person,
company or place.

*

Hamburger again for Marlon.

*

Girl next to me on the
train is reading a fat book
about Proust. Full of over-
sized words and lengthy,
pretentious sentences. All
I can muster is trawling
through text messages
but her frown tells me I'm
having a better read.

The bank still not returning calls including the complaints
department. I couldn't tell you how many times I had to repeat
everything. Six months out and still not any clearer about
what's going on with the overdraft. I couldn't get on to anyone
who could explain processes and procedures or who had the
power to make a decision.

Our lawyer left the firm and we had a new one. He rang me.
Told me to get tougher with the bank. Easier said than done,
especially when they never return my calls.

Three months ago, I bought a
packet of plastic pegs. Every
single one busted.

If the Quakers hadn't invented
the peg, Mum would have.
There isn't anyone on the
planet who has found more
use for a clothes peg than
Mum. She pegs everything –
shade-cloth to a fence or over
a car, tops of freezer bags and
cereal packets, plants together,
notes together, bills together,
calendar pages together,
messages to the front gate.
When I mentioned this to Mum,
she said she has more use for
a curtain ring.

*

Crossed town to State Hockey
Centre. Semi-final. Kids
warming up – all are hitting
the ball like they are striking
a baseball. Shoulder high
whacks. Just got a call from
the Karratha real estate agent.
Third set of tenants leaving.
Now three empty places. Every
single call brings worse news –
every single call.

*

Bloke on phone on train. My
age. Country. His dad has died
too. He's talking to a sibling

about how to sell the family's
cattle.
'Don't be rushed, sit with the
paperwork in front of you.
Make him sweat. Two hours
in the yard, three hours on
paperwork … You have a big
day ahead of you … Where's
Mum? She's not on the tractor,
is she?'

*

Tornado-like winds outside.
A man's coming up the street
with the walk of a greyhound.
Tough, slight sideways sway,
deliberate steps. He has a
small thin face with the wary
but resigned greyhound look.
Reminds me of something I
saw years ago in a back lane
in Quirindi when I went to
visit my grandmother. A bloke
was outside a shed, smoking.
His singlet barely covered
his big, yeasty belly. We
nodded. I heard something
like a motor and looked in the
shed. In the darkness, there
was a greyhound running on a
treadmill. It looked out at me.
Same wretched look.

*

Got the council's rate notices
for Dad's two units. $2,300
each. Plus strata fees for each
unit is nearly $8,000 per year.

*

Never been this stressed. Hard
to function. The fridge stopped
working yesterday. I'm going
to defrost it to see if that fixes
it.
It has to work.
I have been up until 2 am
the last three nights marking
and preparing to go. I leave
tomorrow morning for the
west. Can't see how I can fit
everything in and sleep.

I spent a month preparing paperwork, contacts and appoint-
ments. The logistics needed to leave for ten days was
compounded by the wrench of leaving Marlon. And I didn't
like flying. At all.

The financial ombudsman got back to me. He wrote that Dad
had accepted the premium level applied to each property.

> 'Given that was the situation, there is no information to
> suggest that the insurance premiums had not been disclosed
> or had been misrepresented or incorrectly applied.'

Didn't address the ludicrous amount? How many other insurance companies swindle elderly people?

I look like a hostage victim,
held at gunpoint in the Andes,
whose family have said, 'No' to
paying the ransom.

Chapter 12
The golden orb

September 2016   **Perth and Karratha**

This was the first time I was flying over west by myself. No buffer, no back-up. I felt dread. After a night in Perth, I was to meet the new lawyer the next morning and sign the contracts to have Dad's titles put into my name and then later that afternoon, fly on to Karratha to set up the sales of the two properties that the bank possessed.

> At the airport. Once I
> board, there's simply
> nothing I can do or panic
> about for four hours.
>
> Seated. Window. Woman
> in front of me, 70, pink
> ribbon in a bow tied high
> in her curled hair like
> she's a newborn. Two
> beers and a sandwich
> and I'll be out of it for the
> flight and not spooked
> with what lies ahead.

I opened the door to the hotel room in Perth. My chest tightened and the air thickened. I rang reception from the room and said, 'No window. I have to be moved.'
They said, 'Wait there.'
'No way.'
At the desk, they said, 'You booked a room without a window.'
'Who books a room without a window?'
Turned out anyone who booked a standard room was booking a room without a window.
They said they didn't have a room left but I persisted.
After more keyboard tapping, there was one but the air-conditioner was broken.
'What's the air-con for?'
I wasn't being facetious. I had no idea. The weather was glorious.

I'm in the front bar of an open
pub with a pot of delicious
beer and a plate of calamari. A
beautiful breeze on my face.

*

This morning I opened the
curtains and saw three
skyscrapers – Bankwest, BHP
Billiton and Rio Tinto. Sums up
WA for you.

*

The contracts weren't ready
for signing? Why hadn't I been
told that before I got here?
Apart from that, I was glad

> I met the lawyer. I liked his
> questions.

He asked about the real estate agent, the accountant and communication with the bank. He agreed it was a huge mess. He appreciated the work involved in managing it and I felt reassured he was on my side. Looking back at his questions, I can see he understood better than I did what lay ahead in sorting out Dad's properties.

> Magnificent view from the
> plane all the way here. You
> know when the plane circles
> over the milky Dampier salt
> plains, you're arriving in
> Karratha.

> Landed.

Karratha

Dad's friend Nanette picked me up from the airport. She and Bob looked after Dad's ute at their place. I picked it up, went to the supermarket and pulled into Dad's drive about 8 pm. As the headlights lit up the carport, I saw the biggest spider I had ever seen. Almost left my body.

Everything is huge in the North West.

I went to the Rec Club. Place was near empty as there was a rodeo on over the weekend in Paraburdoo – a town six hours away. I had arranged to meet N from the previous visit. I didn't tell him the time of the flight because I didn't want him to think I wanted, or expected, a lift from the airport.

I was nervous. He was at the Rec Club looking exhausted. It was awkward for both of us but all right. I asked had he told anyone about what had happened last time because judging from the reception at the Club's sign-in book, they knew. He said, 'Yes', and smiled. He had been up since five and had to be up at dawn the next day for work. I drove him home and we planned to meet the following night.

I must have been nervous. In Dad's ute, N said, 'You can drive stick?' I hesitated, confused, before I said, 'Yeah, I learnt to drive in an old Holden. Three on the tree.'

I failed to remember that all my cars for the past 30 years have been manuals.

Next morning:

> The spider is weaving a
> spectacular web from one
> pillar to another – it's
> something else.
> Amazing.
> Quiet and cool morning.
> Lovely. No Internet. I'm sitting
> out the front of Dad's in the
> breeze as he and Marcus did.

That weekend was my first weekend off from online marking for thirteen months. I remember being exhilarated with the freedom and of having nothing pressing to do. There was nothing until Monday when businesses opened and I could resume the online marking on Nanette's computer.

> I went for a drive to Dampier
> and then Hearson Cove.

High tide. The water was ideal.
Dolphin dived for an hour. How
could Dad not have brought
me here.

N cancelled tonight. Texted he
was tired, up early for work
the next day and was going to
have a quiet night in. Shame,
if nothing else, I would have
liked a beer with someone.

Father's Day

I went out to the cemetery at dawn. I had made toast and
a thermos of coffee to have breakfast with Dad. He loved
Father's Day. He'd wait by the phone all day for the four of us
to call.

'Well, looks like one of your brothers beat you to the post.'
'Your sister was the first cab off the rank this year.'
'Someone got up early ... earlier than you.'

The soil had settled over his grave. We had the cemetery to
ourselves. I was there all morning, walking around, tidying up
some graves and talking to him. He had thrown me into his
world. It was a comfort to feel he was with me. I told him how
things were going and how it will be ok. I cried a lot.

Now back at Dad's with the
spider. My, she's something
else. Apparently, she's an orb
spider. A golden orb.

> Restless. Need to do
> something.

> At Point Samson. The drive
> was beautiful – the desert
> wildflowers are out. Hadn't
> expected that. I drove over
> the bridge of the estuary. Tide
> rushing out. Wanted fish and
> chips first and then I'll go back
> there. Ordered garlic prawns
> for Dad.

I wanted to be around people that day but Father's Day at Point Samson without Dad, or anyone from the family, was lonely. On the verandah of Samson Beach Tavern, I thought about how Dad had made the decision to stay in the Pilbara. He was never going to live in Sydney – he saw cities as ant nests – and to return to northern New South Wales was not an option.

The Pilbara was big enough to put the past behind him and to give him a new life but, as his daughter, I saw the struggles and the sacrifices and the toll of decades of living on his own had had upon him.

Dad had sensibilities and interests that he could not express up there. Before he went west, he had sung in a men's choir and read books by Ring Lardner, Angus Wilson and Philip Roth. He watched movies by Jacques Tati and Peter Sellers and had dreamt of becoming a vet and later of being a permaculturist in Queensland.

> At the estuary. Tide turning.
> Coming in. Local family – three

> generations – fishing for
> barramundi off the rocks.

Every morning Dad's Aboriginal neighbour, S, greeted me with the same gentle salute and the occasional, 'I miss the old fella' or 'I miss the old man.'

He had the most relaxed, languid walk of anyone I've ever seen. Beautiful.

> Wish I walked like that. Makes
> me feel I scurry.

> Ever seen Richard Pryor
> mimic an indignant white man
> walking stiff-legged past people
> who he considered to be in
> the way: 'You wanna move out
> of the way fellas, excuse me,
> thank you very much ... Takin'
> up all the fucking area, Jesus
> Christ.'
> Gold. Dad, in a fury, to a tee.

A good friend of Dad's called in to say hello and see if I needed anything. Terry. I liked him. Easy to talk to. I liked how he liked Dad so much. He understood Dad was a dreamer. I suspect he was too.

> Back at Dad's. Long day. Went
> to the council about overdue
> rates and underground power
> bills, real estate agent about
> the sales, and priced some
> things at the hardware shop.

Expensive up here. Not great
in this house. Had fitful night's
sleep – new sounds I can't
make out. Lists of things I still
have to do this week running
through my head.

I had a look inside Dad's Spanish house – exposed dark brick
walls, long narrow hallway and big arches. Casa Blanca – the
first house up for sale.

I'm not sure Dad could have comprehended the enormity of
what I had to do. He thought he could live out the bust, hang
in there until another boom. There's a foolproof plan.

Terry called. He wants to
contact the mechanic in Dad's
industrial yard to see if he
wants to buy a shed to put
up there. What? What if the
mechanic sees this as an
opportunity to put the shed
up somewhere else? The
mechanic is the only reliable
source of income. Why would
we create a situation where
he might want to leave? And
I'm not moving another man's
piece of junk.

Going for a swim.

Archaeologists have found
evidence of Aboriginal people
on Rosemary Island off

Dampier Archipelago going
back to the end of the last ice
age.

Terry told me the rocks out
on Burrup Peninsula are two
billion years old.

He reckons his wife says the
same thing about 'no more
men's junk.' Oh my God, just
saw a grasshopper land in the
orb spider's web, struggle free
and drop to the ground. Still
there, stunned.

I was barracking for it. I
thought, Oh no, what have I
done leaving the porch light on.
The web is full of moths and
beetles wrapped up like little
mummies. You've never seen
such a gleeful spider.

I saw N one night at his place. Extreme level of exhaustion
that felt like he needed hospitalisation. Almost comatose.
Something was up. He was a different man. I was surprised
to feel unwelcome. He was upset. He talked about an incident
with his manager – a capricious micro-manager. He was told
to get his hands out of his pockets in front of female staff. I
didn't know why he took it on but I guess, maybe, the final
straw in a long line of small humiliations. The manager
tracked his company vehicle with mobile phone surveillance
that sounded almost illegal. I wanted to give him a hug but he
didn't want me there so I left.

Not good to see a big bloke
let managerial pettiness
undermine him like that. Long
work shifts, exhaustion and
worry about job stability don't
help. Skews anyone's emotions.

*

Tough on their own. After
three years on their own, in
this town, most blokes should
leave. They are in the danger
zone of never leaving.

Hard not to feel I'm starring
in my own version of *Wake in
Fright*.

I definitely felt a *Wake in Fright* element in being an out-of-towner in Karratha. A lot of attitudes, assumptions and grievances in a remote mining town in hot, dry country are alien to me.

I often wondered how Dad coped with the harsh expectations to conform to a gruelling work life of early starts, hard physical work in blazing heat that was often seven days a week, and lights out by nine. Truth was, he loved to make money.

I'm about to head down the
North West Coastal Highway
to a swimming hole on the
Nullagine River. Miaree Pond.
Hoping it's the place Dad took
me 30 years ago.

It is. I remember the river as
a lake. Shady banks, deep
water, reeds, swarms of
insects, water birds.
Otherworldly colours. I
remember Dad talking to a
friend as I swam. I remember
Dad smiling on the way home
that I had loved the place.

*

I woke at 1 am, to men with torches, shouting and running
through the carport between the ute and my bedroom window.
Lights flashed around the bedroom walls and lit the room up
like a pinball machine. Oh Jesus, I thought, they think this
place is abandoned. They are going to break in. I heard them
run down the side of the house and around the back. Dad's
place didn't have fences. I grabbed my phone and snuck down
the hall. My heart pounded. Do I let them know someone's
here? Then I realised it was the police and an Aboriginal teenager. The cops ran after him after he took off when he saw the
cop car. The teenager hadn't done anything. Everyone relaxed.
I could hear them talking about someone they all knew and his
connection to an incident the previous week. I went back to
bed but took hours to fall asleep.

S's whipper snipping the
front lawn. Terrified of
snakes. Fair enough, summer
before last a plumber was
fixing a drain in Dad's
backyard and a tiger snake
bit him. Serious. Had to be
flown to Perth.

Little sleep. S and his mates
were tearing into each
other out on the street for
most of the night. Calling
each other fucking useless
black bastards and that
they were worthless and
no good. Awful stuff about
themselves. Terrible.
Language of troubled,
traumatised men.
And now, he's back to his
soft, showered, sober self,
waves good morning, 'Miss
the old fella.'
'Yeah, me too,' I say as he
saunters down to his mate's
house.

*

It's getting hot. Very hot.
How do people function in
this relentless heat?
Cleaning Casa Blanca for
its sale. Had a swim in
the cove after six hours of
marking assignments. After
this, back to the council to
sort out a payment plan for
the rates and underground
power costs.

*

Love to see the rock art again
but nervous about snakes out
there.

*

I've made the golden orb the
happiest spider in the country.
Fluoro lights burning above
her for most nights this week.
She's fucking huge. Should
see her frenzy over the moths
coming in tonight.

She's frantically wrapping
moths, beetles, anything that
is stuck in her web but is
desperate to keep returning to
the middle and remain stock
still to wait for something else
to land. She's out of her mind.

She's back in the middle. Still
as a post. As if hiding. Another
grasshopper got caught but
managed to break free. Now a
beetle is stuck. She races over
to wrap it. She's done it.

The suitor's behind a brick pillar
to the right, down low, above a
bucket of cement, languishing
in a shabby little broken web.

> She's spectacular. Didn't think I
> could feel like this over a spider.
> Imagine spraying or stomping
> on something like that.

I texted N again to ask if we could meet. I wanted to leave on good terms and for it not to be awkward at the Rec Club. It was already hard to walk in there. But he asked me to leave it be. He wrote that he wasn't my toy. Toy? It stung but I hadn't a clue what he was talking about. I sent a final text. Thanked him for the previous visit and that I appreciated his kindness and that's what had stayed with me.

I went to the Rec Club to watch the AFL finals game between West Coast and Western Bulldogs. I couldn't sit another night in Dad's house, alone. We had given Dad's TV away. All I could see around me was what had to be done to the place. Fucking everything. Terry came with me for a short while. Always better to walk into the Rec Club with someone. He knew that and offered. After he left, a young bloke included me in his family's conversations and I had a good night.

> Lots of West Coast supporters
> in brand new jerseys. A few
> bum-bags. Can't get enough of
> the barrage of insults at their
> own team as they get trounced.
> 'Have a fuckin' shot,
> FUCKHEAD.'
> 'We know you've got the ball,
> ya fucking dumb cunt. DO
> SOMETHING.'
> 'Played the whole game like
> he's fuckin' cross-eyed.'

They've really turned on their
team.

*

The golden orb hasn't moved
from the middle of her web
since last night. She had a
grasshopper wrapped next to
her that was the size of a little
finger. It's gone. Not on the
web or the ground. The web
isn't in its usual splendid shape.
Worried.

One reason I went up to the Pilbara was to introduce myself to
some of the people I had dealt with, and will be dealing with,
on the phone. Also, to find out the cost of things and to understand how things work up here but the world was so different
from mine, a week wasn't enough. I saw how money and/or
pride play big roles in most interactions.

The orb spider hasn't moved all
day. Dead. The web is a broken
mess. So upsetting. I left the
lights on to attract moths. I
indulged her. I killed her.

*

I can't stay in at Dad's tonight.
Depressing. No comfort. No
furniture. No floor. No orb.
I want to go to the Rec Club
to watch another footy game.

> I don't feel welcome but I want
> to be around people.
>
> Whacky circumstances mean
> their sense of me is of my
> father. They don't understand
> me but they knew him.
>
> In ways I never did ... I have
> no idea how I am seen other
> than the assumption Dad was
> worth a fortune and, as his
> daughter, so am I. My only
> assets are a reliable 13-year-
> old Corolla hatchback, a speedy
> kid, a damn good suitcase and
> a sweet-tempered dog.
>
> I guess they think I waltz into
> the club, like I do into town.
> Waltz in, waltz out. But doesn't
> feel like that for me. More like
> hard paddling than a silky glide.

N and I saw each other at the Rec Club but he was out the back
in the beer garden so I stayed inside. He looked pained but I
could be sensing that just to feel less alone, less unwelcome,
less stung.

> Can't see the regulars who I
> like a lot and who make me
> feel welcome. Must be outside.
> Don't feel I can go out there.
> This ain't easy. I feel Dad's
> absence. His stool is empty.

Relieved to see the footy game
has started.

I got a beer, looked around again for a familiar face and saw J, the pool player. He was in his work clothes watching the game. I was so pleased to see him. He had crossed my mind often in Melbourne. His response, when I said hello, was less enthusiastic. I suspect he had seen me before I saw him. He kept saying he was leaving after the next quarter and then the next quarter but I felt he wasn't going anywhere.

Hawthorn versus Geelong. Another finals game. I sat next to him but after some time, his housemate came back to the table, drunk, and said, 'That's my chair.'
I got up to leave, thinking rude prick.
J said, 'Sit here.'
And I moved to a chair on the other side of him.

Our conversation loosened. He relaxed. The electric link we had shared the first night returned. I saw how he had gotten under my skin. He invited me to his house. Outside I told him I was 20 years older. He said he didn't care. He said he had wished and hoped for my return. A declaration that moved and frightened me.

What happened between us is our story. But we ran from each other. He ran to his house, and I ran to the ute. Maybe because of misunderstandings. Or awkwardness. Or too much vulnerability. Or a clash of vulnerabilities. Or an understanding it was never to be.

When I got back to Dad's, I wanted to get out of my skin.

The orb? Not moving. Dead.
Terrible.

I feel dreadful about the spider.
She was magnificent.

Packing up. Totally over this
town. Hot, empty, unhealthy,
unwelcoming. Ready to come
home.

In my darkest frustrated
moments, it's hard not to see
this town as cobbled together
by dreamers, opportunists and
runaways.

One dream came true.
Yesterday the young baby-
faced truck driver who I had
met during my last visit, got
his licence to drive road trains.
He was in the Rec Club last
night, beaming. Today he
starts a new job driving the big
rigs.

I had to tell the family we were selling Dad's house. I wasn't
prepared to spend money on it from afar. It was well beyond
a quick makeover. Everything needed attention. I had to keep
turning off the water as I heard it pooling under the house.
Exorbitant prices for material and for labour. Daunting sums
of money. Impossible to know who to trust from the other
side of the country. I couldn't let this drag on for years. It was
already too much for Marlon and me.

Yesterday S's wife returned
from two weeks cooking in

a remote mining camp. Two
weeks on, two weeks off.
They fought on the front lawn
showing the tensions and clash
of expectations inherent in this
work set-up.

Today they have spent the day
walking around the streets
together as quiet as church
mice.

To tread that softly.

On my last night I went to say goodbye to J before going to
Nanette and Bob's for dinner. The night before we had parted
saying that's what I would do. The front door was open.
Through the screen door I saw him in his work clothes sitting
out the back. I knocked. He dived off his chair and out of sight.
A housemate came to the door and said J was at the pub. I
wasn't interested in catching him out. His reaction didn't
carry any thought.

Pure panic. Pure flight.

I went over to Nanette and Bob's on the other side of town.
Nanette and I sat out the back and I told her about the estate's
situation. She said, every Sunday Dad drove over to sit with
Bob and watch *Songs of Praise* yet he had told them nothing
about his financial mess. We discussed the difficulties of
dealing with banks. She said not all banks are uncooperative
and not all banks continue to charge interest and fees on a
dead person's debt. She told me of people who had bought
their places in the boom and then overnight lost their jobs and
their worlds turned upside down.

Nanette worked at the Pilbara Community Legal Services (PCLS). I hadn't known she was an accredited financial counsellor and at the time of the bust, the chief executive officer of PCLS. Nanette was at the coalface of the mining bust. She knew how mortgage stress and financial ruin could destroy individuals and families. She worked hard to alleviate the untenable situation for many and to help them deal with their debts and the banks and to get on with their lives. Dad's pride would've stopped him telling her of his financial circumstances. I saw why he admired Nanette so much – her intellect and her commitment to the region and its people. And why he would have been scared to tell her. She would have told him to stop getting loans and to sell.

Last day

I wrote a short letter to J, put it in his mailbox and went back to Dad's. I felt agitated and then embarrassed. The letter was glib. I went back to get it but it was gone. Either J or the wind had taken it.

I had made light of what had happened between us. I wrote of an image I had seen earlier that morning at the Karratha lookout. A man with his back to the sunrise, and warmth, who sat staring lovingly at a tower, as the sun hit and lit up its metal frame. Describing the image was a distraction from writing how I felt. Our connection had been cut short and I felt rattled that we hadn't parted well.

I didn't find anything light and breezy about the single men in Karratha. Maybe with each other, after a few beers, but not with me, a woman from out of town. They were quick to feel slighted or injured and to retreat. To run away. I was surprised how quickly their emotional responses resembled each other's.

I saw moments on their faces where they looked pained and at a loss.

Of course, I'm describing my father. The men I spent time with, or even talked to, were all versions of my father. Single, sensitive and unresolved. Emotional. Heavy-hearted. They lived thousands of miles from where they'd grown up. They wanted to be part of a world bigger than themselves. The men weren't cocky. They were raw. I liked that they wore their heart on their sleeve. I liked them.

My final text to N and my letter to J were more for me than for them.

I realised they would be relieved to see the back of me.

I pictured them scrambling over the white plastic chairs in the beer garden to get away from me. Conjuring up that picture often threw me into a tailspin.

The texts and the letter were my way of gaining peace of mind. I wanted to clear up misunderstandings. I didn't want their experience with me to compound any shitty perceptions of the world or of women. I wanted there to be goodwill.

I wanted us all to be braver. To be more courageous. Like I had wanted Dad to be and like I wanted myself to be. All of us.

*

On my last morning, I thought, I can't stand to leave the dead spider dangling and her web in tatters, so I decided to take it down. I grabbed a bit of the web and she moved.

She isn't dead. She's just
completely stuffed. Gorged. So
happy she's alive.

The orb spider had her fill. She needed a rest. She was exhausted.

I used to have a school ruler
embossed with wild flowers of
WA.

Red and black Sturt Desert Pea
is everywhere. Dad's favourite.
A wilful plant. Only grows
where it wants to grow. Often
in the gravel on the side of the
road. Not seen one in a front
garden. A small victory if you
can manage it. Nanette has
metres of it in her backyard.

On my way to the airport, Nanette and I went to the cemetery for Dad's birthday. He would have been 78. We both arrived with Sturt Desert Pea. I had picked some from the side of the road and Nanette brought a cutting from her backyard to plant on the grave. Terry came too, to say goodbye. Dad's friend Bob stayed home. Like Dad, he's an emotional man. It was too painful for Bob to see the grave. I'm sure Dad would have responded in the same way had the situation been reversed. Dad would have loved that the three of us were out there, in good spirits, for his birthday.

As the plane flew south over the salt plains and the town disappeared, I thought of Dad on his own and of his real friends who wanted nothing from him but friendship.

Chapter 13
Sunday calls

During my early 30s, when I lived on my own in St Kilda, I wrote:

That's Me

I read a short piece by Lydia Davis about a character who no one ever rang. She couldn't check her answer machine because she hadn't left the house but if she did leave the house, she could come home and check the answer machine.

Ha. That's me. I do that. I go out to come back in and see if the red light is flashing. Ha, that's why I'm here in the library. I get in a deep bath, too, and keep my head underwater and only get out when the water has turned cold to see if the red light is flashing. I've done it for years. I smile and nod. Years. And then I see the piece's title, 'Lonely'.

*

I didn't see myself as lonely. I had moved from Sydney to Melbourne to do a Post Graduate Diploma in Animation. During that time, Dad rang me on Sundays and we often talked for hours on our landlines.

Dad and I did the small talk – comparing weather or our take on something we had heard or seen or on an anecdote or story someone had told one of us, and we talked deeply. Dad didn't baulk from my questions. He didn't initiate them, but he always answered them truthfully and with sincerity.

During one call I remember Dad saying, 'It sounds like someone thinks her old man is weak.'
To which I replied, 'He could be braver.'

Another time I said, 'Why do you think we always felt we had to do so well at school? God, the tension trying to impress you.'

He was silent for a few moments and then said, 'You should never have to impress a deserter.'

Maybe Dad was lonely. Maybe Dad needed those conversations too. Maybe having them showed he was braver than I gave him credit for. He'd call and I always picked up the phone.

*

Recently I told a friend that my father and I used to talk a lot on the phone. I said sometimes we talked about him leaving us.

She said, 'What did he say?'

I tried to respond but realised I couldn't. I stumbled over an awkward answer.

She asked again, 'But what did he say?'

I said he called himself a deserter and that he said he lost his light when he lost his family.

'It was so selfish,' she said.

It gave me a jolt to hear the word 'selfish' and to see I couldn't give my friend, or myself, the answer she wanted. I hadn't used the word 'selfish' to describe Dad. I used the word 'cowardly', because then I could tell myself that I was still in his thoughts – still in the picture.

On the phone Dad and I had talked of his loss. We never spoke of my mother's loss or my brothers' or mine. We didn't talk about how the light went out for us too. I asked Dad questions but I protected him, and me, from the truth of what the upheaval of him leaving had meant for his family. And he never asked. At the time, however, the phone calls were enough for the two of us.

Chapter 14
Running two lives

September–November 2016   Melbourne

> Terry let me know that the orb
> spider was still out the front of
> Dad's.

Back in Melbourne, I went on running two lives – my Melbourne life with Marlon and my life as the executor of Dad's estate. The two properties – a house (Casa Blanca) and a duplex – owned by the bank were up for sale. I was setting up the sale of the third property – the corrugated-iron house – for the estate to pay off other debts.

> Going to Officeworks to scan
> and photocopy documents for
> estate's lawyer. Shit, forgot
> my purse. All this, on top of
> hours of online marking. Eight
> assignments came in last night.

*

Melbourne: look out the
window to see the sun is
shining, grab the dog lead, call
Remy and walk out the door
into hail.

I love the sudden and
unexpected changes in the
weather.

*

My house is a write-off and the
front yard and back yard – oh
God. All I can see is the work
needed to be done. The only
time I can imagine factoring
in time to garden is at night
under street lights. Fire up the
mower at 1 am, bring out the
whipper-snipper at 3 am and
onto the hedge by dawn.

*

The backyard is mowed. Feels
so good to turn off the mower,
step back and see it look as
open and restful as a golf
course.

Gave the hibiscus another flat
top.

*

Here's an experience I've never had before: An attractive gardener working across the road asked me out when I was mowing out the front. We met for ten, 15, minutes, yet later that day, he texted of 'our emotional connection' and drove back in his ute to put a small bouquet of flowers he had made in my mailbox. It smelt exquisite but good God, it's like something off *The Bachelor*. I thought those men worked off a script.
His marriage had recently ended. Spinning badly.
I have to nip it in the bud.

*

At last, a good phone call. A developer is flying in to check out the duplex and put in an offer. Cash in 14 days if we accept. I'm not getting my hopes up ... too high.

*

Today I need to contact the lawyer about contracts for the houses to be in my name that were supposed to be written up a month ago. Infuriating.

People should let you know
when they are snowed under
and too busy to do things in a
timely fashion. I can't think of
one time when I haven't had to
chase something up. Wait, do
I get charged for them to read
those emails?

*

Tonight I watched a dogged
little ant struggle with a grain
of cooked rice. After five
minutes of covering half an
inch of the table, other ants
came to help. They moved the
grain to the edge of the table.
They bundled together and
went over the edge still holding
onto it. They moved along the
side of the table. I thought, let
it drop, let it fall. Go on and
then run down the table leg to
get it.
After another minute or so,
as they continued to move in
small vertical circles, I got up,
turned on the lamp for them,
turned off the ceiling light and
left them to it. They had a long
night ahead.

October

Seven months in, and still the affairs of the estate occupied nearly all my time.

> Upsetting day. Saw my artless
> life. I've gone on hold, my
> social life has gone on hold,
> the house is on hold and I
> have to fight not to let Marlon
> go on hold.

> Thoughts racing – too many
> planes coming in to land. Crash
> land. Not great for sleep.
> For years and years, I had
> nightmares most nights – two
> or three – but after my last
> Karratha trip that changed. I
> don't know why. Maybe seeing
> Marlon organised and ok with me
> being away has something to do
> with it.

The nightmares had been gruesome. What started as an ordinary situation suddenly turned violent. Danger struck and I was about to be shot, stabbed, pushed off a cliff, sucked into a bottomless pit, run over by a truck, trapped under a falling wall, hit by a train, crushed by a tidal wave, lose Marlon in a crowd of thousands, or be thrown from a high-rise balcony and so on.

Once on the phone, I told Dad about my nightmares and he said, 'All my dreams are exhilarating – like being at a carnival.'

I found that hard to believe.

At baseball – a woman is doing
vaguely obscene stretches
next to a team of kids. What
happens to a woman's mind
when she wears active wear in
public?

She won't stop. I'm not the
only one watching. The kids
are giving her a wide berth.
Who exercises like that at
their kid's baseball game? For
everyone's sake, especially
your kid's, go to a gym and get
on a contraption.

Marlon would have told me
off if I tried to pull a stunt like
that.

*

We drive all over Melbourne
to playing grounds – footy,
hockey and baseball – and
it always surprises me when
we move away from the bay,
how often, from roads and
playing fields, I can see the
Dandenong hills in the distance.

*

Heading to Officeworks to
print off forms, fill them in,
sign them and then re-scan
documents. Wow, there's
someone in Cuban heels. I
had Cuban heels in the '90s.
Came as a blow once when I
realised the only other person
at Sydney airport in Cuban-
heeled boots was Derryn Hinch.

*

The developer put in a pitifully
low offer on the duplex – cash.
A joke. Marcus says he needs a
bigger suitcase.

Sent counter offer on another
property: the corrugated-iron
house. Fingers crossed.

*

Sent letters to the lawyer and
to the bank. May accept an
offer today on the corrugated-
iron house. Ok, not great but
ok. I'm marking and waiting
for the real estate agent to call
soon. Marlon having trouble
with Shakespeare. I couldn't
work it out at school either.

It's impossible to read
Shakespeare until you have
your heart broken, been
betrayed, screwed over,
worked for assholes, met
deviants and been involved
with a few psychopaths. Insight
required. And know something
about language. In fact, it's
hilarious.

First property. The duplex. Sold. Only eight to go.

Thanks for the invitation but I
can't today as I need to make
calls and send emails to hurry
the bank and lawyer along.
Nothing is straight forward.

*

Sorry I can't tonight – six
assignments to mark.

*

An online student sent me an
email starting:
Dear Mrs Trevitt
In my message back to her, I
wrote, 'Call me Annette.'
She messaged back:
Dear Trevitt
Thank you again! My second
assessment will be finished

soon.
After that I signed off all my
correspondence to her:
Regards,
Trevitt

*

Have a worryingly huge day
ahead. Some problems arising
in the estate about missing
property titles so anchored to
the photocopier at Officeworks.

All I want is for lights to start
lining up in the tunnel.

Dad had two vacant blocks in New South Wales. One was a small block in Blandford that he bought in 1991. At the time the block had a small wooden house on it but that's long gone. Nine years ago, Dad tried to sell the vacant block and found out that his purchase of the block had never been registered at the New South Wales Land Title Office, even though he had paid council rates since 1991. A lawyer in that region had searched for the title of deeds but couldn't find it. The bank said they didn't have the title. Dad gave up.

I knew this was going to be an issue that I had to sort out. A lawyer quoted a fee in the range of $4,400 to $8,800 to find the title and to reseal the grant of probate in New South Wales. I didn't want to pay that. There wasn't any money in the estate and I didn't have four-plus grand so I had to find the title myself.

I called everyone in the white pages with the surname of the previous owner to try and find him and ask if he had any evidence of the sale or if he could sign a Statutory Declaration that he had sold it to Dad. One woman asked if I wanted her to contact her son in ASIO. After a dozen calls all over the country, and exhausting all possibilities, I came to the conclusion that he must have moved to a nursing home or off the grid or he had died.

Had some luck. I went through Dad's papers again and found a house insurance receipt for the block in NSW dated 1997 and on it, wait for it, interested parties: the bank. The fucking bank has the title of deeds. I know it.

*

The orb spider is still at Dad's. I've been reading about golden orbs and people's tales of their pet orb. People are so attached. An orb can live from a year to 18 months. She's at least six months old.

*

I had accepted an offer on the duplex. Having a difficult time with the bank releasing the titles for the two properties

that they own: Casa Blanca
and the duplex.

That's it. Should tell them I just
had a haircut and now ready to
front up for an interview on *A
Current Affair.*

Is that show still on air?

*

Someone made an offer on
Casa Blanca. $200,000. I'm
not selling that low. We need
at least $250,000 to help cover
the overdraft. It needs work,
and is pretty dated but it's big.
Real estate told me no one
wants that street?

Terry checked the street. Said
nothing to complain about
in that street. Lots of land
cruisers and boats.

November

The sale of the duplex fell through. The interested party
couldn't get a loan. And the person who put in an offer on
Casa Blanca withdrew it.

This could drag on for years.
I took my frustration of the

first two property sales falling
through out on the backyard.
Set the lawn mower blades low
and hit tufts of grass hard. Dirt
flew everywhere. The backyard
looks better but it took a
beating.

I'm having a day away from
banks, lawyers, real estate
agents and lawn mowers. At
least one sale had felt like
something was shifting. I need
to, as Richard Pryor said, 'Get
some sunshine on my face.'

Chapter 15
Detective skin

November–December 2016   **Melbourne**

The two properties connected to the overdraft were back on the market.

> A magpie is low in the sky, over flapping and covering very little air space. Like a little kid who can't swim.

>   *

> I am jumping out of my detective skin. Today I received in the mail a piece of paper that nine years ago couldn't be found – a rates notice from 1991 to say Dad was about to purchase a block in NSW and the name of three solicitors. One step closer to finding out why the title of the block was never registered.

After five calls to regional councils up there, I found someone who listened – Brenda. I told her the story of the unregistered title of deeds and then, unbeknownst to me, she asked a group of women in another council building to go through archive boxes dated 1991 and there it was. The rates notice that proved Dad was the impending buyer of the block.

I contacted one of the solicitors on the notice. I had contacted him before as he still worked in the region, to see what he knew – nothing, until now. His signature was the one on the notice. I wasn't accusing him. Most likely the bank had failed to register Dad on the title. He was going to try and track down the files. I was out of my detective-fucking mind with this.

> At a hockey game in Berwick.
> Everyone is getting into
> position. Marlon's on the wing.
>
> I love Brenda. Unsung council
> hero. She saves me hours of
> work and saved us thousands.

The solicitor couldn't find any files on the sale of the block. Back to the bank. I refused to hear 'No' from the bank about that lost title. I knew Dad. I knew the bank. They had it.

I sent through a form requesting a search in the bank for the lost title. A week later, I got a call from the bank to say the New South Wales Land Title Office didn't have the title. I rang the bank.

'Dear God, we know that,' I said. 'That's why I put in a request. We can't find the title because the bank never registered it at Land Title Office.'
He couldn't grasp it.

I said, 'I can't speak any plainer.'

After half an hour of going through it step by step by step, he seemed to grasp the situation. The following week, the bank sent an email to say they needed the title to authorise the Land Title Office to sign off on it.

My swearing reached new heights. I rang with barely contained fury. I got on to a woman. She got it straight away but had no power to act. So often the case in the bank.

'My father was a creature of habit,' I said. 'He banked with your bank. The bank has the title. Please. Please. Get someone smart and over 50 to find it.'

She did. She got P in Sydney. He found the original and a copy. I fuckin' knew it.

The title of deeds was with Dad's other title deeds in the Perth office and had been the whole time. The title was an old system New South Wales title but the opening sentence was:

> THIS DEED made the 10th day of October, One thousand nine hundred and ninety one BETWEEN J ... S ..., formerly of Murrurundi but now of Bathurst in the State of New South Wales, ... of the one part AND RICHARD JOHN TREVITT of Karratha in the State of Western Australia (hereinafter called the "purchaser") ...

> P sent the original title to the
> Land Title Office. You can tell
> by his voice, his tone, he is
> trustworthy and thorough.
> Can't tell you the anguish all
> that had caused Dad.

*

Soon I will have the title for
the resealing of probate in
NSW.

*

Flat out. Assignments
appearing on my screen like
Pokémons.

*

At Marlon's baseball practice
on the sideline of the diamond.
Humongous, dark clouds
coming in low over the bay.
Boulders rumbling. Any minute,
a downpour.

*

Terry dropped in to check on
Dad's house and the spider.
She has moved to the western
side of the house. Heart-
warming to picture her swaying
on a cool south westerly.

One morning I made three calls:

First call – Shares.

I rang the stockbroker to ask where was the money from the sale of Dad's shares. The stockbroker didn't know. He would look into it. Should have been in the account two weeks ago.

Second call – The bank.
The usual.

Third call – Super.
Two months earlier, I sent in the paperwork to claim Dad's super. A few thousand. Rang a month later and was told it was being processed. I rang and was told they have been waiting for a certified copy of his death certificate. I checked the photocopies of the paperwork I had sent and saw I had sent it. They lost it. Before I knew that, I asked why hadn't anyone called or emailed to tell me that's why there was a hold-up?

How could the department that issued death benefits and dealt with the bereaved be so careless?

Every time I phoned, I spoke to someone different, yet every time they called me the same thing – my father's executioner.

> Need to go up the street to
> organise another certified copy
> of the death certificate because
> the chemist who certified the
> last one did it but the stamp
> was so smudged no one can
> read it. The original is in Perth
> and I need him to redo the
> smudged copy. He doesn't
> seem to have a problem
> stamping documents lying on
> the top of pens, pill packets
> and prescription pads.

I sent it off. It's done. I need
to get shit out of my life fast.
Because, given the situation,
there's always more shit
around the corner.

*

At work, we're trying to
decipher long-winded emails
from the managerial chain.
Managers we have never met.
Totally incoherent sentences
loaded up with '*key processes*'
and '*ongoing initiatives*'
'*learning outcomes as we move
forward into the future*'.
Ironically, they are closing
down the writing course.

*

On the train I saw an ad,
'Donate your car to prevent
youth homelessness.'
At first I thought it meant
donate your car for homeless
youth to sleep in.

*

Did my taxes. My accountant
is the opposite of a plodder.
To watch her think as she
clicks on her keyboard with

her immaculate nails is like
watching one of those X-ray
light boxes light up.

I received a letter from the coroner in Western Australia to let
me know they were still trying to determine the cause of the
death of my brother, Richard John Trevitt.

December

Another offer on Casa Blanca.
Marcus and I have an uncanny
way of arriving at exactly the
same amount that we think
is reasonable for a place. We
think 25K more.

We put in a counter offer of
20k more.

*

Looks like we sold Casa Blanca.
Time for a tequila, amigo.

*

Sold for a song, no, a jingle,
but at least a house is sold.

I don't know why but as I wandered up my street – beautiful
balmy summer afternoon – I decided to go into another bank
to see if they had any accounts in Dad's name. Earlier this
year, the lawyer had sent out letters to all major banks asking

if Dad had an account with them. I assumed, as I hadn't heard anything, that nothing had come out of the mail-out.

I told the woman at the counter I was the executor of Dad's estate and asked if he had an account with them.
She tapped away.
'Yes.'
'What, you do?'

I filled out the necessary forms and waited. They found a security package.

The deeds for his house.

I hadn't found them at his house and was putting off the paperwork to get a copy. I wanted to cry with the ease of finding that package. A Christmas gift. There wasn't any record of receiving the letter from the lawyer.

> I spent the day Xmas shopping.
> Was in a carpark loading
> my car and turned to see
> the shopping trolley hurtling
> towards parked cars. Got to
> it just before it hit a pricey
> European taillight. Then went
> to another shopping centre.
> Once there, I couldn't work
> out why I was there. Went
> inside, came out ten minutes
> later, empty-handed, to find no
> car. Instead, a big sign on the
> wall saying, 'Reserved Parking.
> Cars may be towed away.' After
> minutes of confusion, I realised

I was on the wrong level.
Christmas, never enjoyed the
lead-up to it.

*

Standing in the train thinking,
Jesus, your 50s are so relaxing.

Now I get why young people
say, 'I want to retire by 30.'
They have seen their worn-out
parents.

*

On the train heading out to
Zone 2. Had to come out here
for a compulsory in-house
professional development day,
otherwise we have been told
'we can't teach next year.'
A common threat.

We had to sit in front of one PowerPoint presentation after
another. Unbearable. Who can follow text-heavy slides, let
alone remember the verb-free content? The language. The
slides might as well have been written in Hungarian. During
the second presentation, everyone moved towards their
phones. Fifteen minutes in and no one was listening. Excruci-
ating to witness the whole thing.

On our lunch break I walked
past the student counselling
services. Imagine being

outside the door, suicidal, and
you see this poster set in three
different fonts:
Happiness *can be found even
in the darkest times, if one only
remembers* to turn on the light.

*

Every call to the bank is like
ramming my head into the side
of a huge immoveable beast.

*

Merry Christmas to you all.

*

I can't get clear answers from
anyone at the bank about the
release of the titles on the
houses the bank own. Worried
as I don't want to jeopardise
the sale of Casa Blanca in
January.

Painful to catch yourself mid-
sentence, shrill with despair.

Feels like an endless maze of
delays.

I've had two sleepless nights
over this.

*

Sorry I missed your call.
Madness of miscommunication
took up the day.

Finally, I spoke to a really
helpful person, L, at the
bank. The first one to get the
situation and respond with
action – waiting for a call back
as he's trying to sort things out.
Incredible to feel he's listening,
to be heard. Teary with relief.
Christmas. Can't wait for
January the first. Favourite
day of the year. Festive
expectations are over and all to
look forward to is ahead.

*

This was our first Christmas without Dad in 15 years. Once
Marlon was born, that was it – he always arrived for Christmas
Day. Often without telling me the day or time of his arrival.
Once my brother texted to tell me the eagle was set to land in
Melbourne that evening. 7 pm, Christmas Eve.

I'll miss Dad. It's not Christmas
without him on the couch,
under the lamp, in a nest of
newspapers and crossword
books, and looking up to say,
'another coffee when you're
ready.'

*

One Christmas, Dad gave
me a big book of Calvin and
Hobbes cartoons. He loved
them. I love that he loved
the adorable duo. Whenever
I read over some of the
cartoons, I think of the photo
of Dad and his teddy that his
mother ditched when he was
two. His Hobbes.

Years ago, one morning, a man in his 70s pushing an old
Emmaljunga pram got on the train. He looked a lot like Dad.
I pulled down the seat beside me and beckoned him over. He
sat down. A cream baby blanket hung over the hood of the
pram and covered what was in it. We talked. I asked where
he lived. 'A boarding house,' he said. He went on to tell me he
was in a drawn-out battle with the State Trustees. As the city
appeared to our right, I asked what was in the pram. He lifted
the blanket gently over the hood and there in the pram, sitting
up and facing him, were two teddy bears. Clean, cared-for
teddy bears. He had tucked them up in blankets. He held on to
the handle of the pram and stared into their button eyes. You
could feel the love go both ways.

I put up the Christmas tree
for Dad. He had loved it,
especially at night. Even in
his 70s, a lit-up Xmas tree
enchanted him. Left him
bright-eyed. Wonder struck.

Chapter 16
The seal

January–February 2017   Melbourne

Marlon and I were heading to Merimbula for a holiday but before we left, I had to make sure Landgate was transmitting the titles of Dad's properties into my name especially for the sale of Casa Blanca on the 20th of January.

Happy New Year

Got five texts today from WA's Water Corporation threatening legal action for five properties. Computer generated but still throws you. Spoke to a woman to sort out a new payment plan/deadline.

I felt miserable until I went to a café, found the cryptic crossword in the paper and saw this clue: Adhere to non-returning boomerang. Answer: Stick.

*

I'm marking. A student's
strategy to ensure she is sitting
at her desk ergonomically:
ensure the weight of my head
is properly supported by my
neck at all times.

*

In the city, wishing the fashion
was different. Too much fabric,
too many busy floral prints and
far too much yellow.

*

A friend texted me about a
clothes shop in the city for
women over 35 at exactly
the same time I was buying
a dusty red tee-shirt. On
the front, Daisy Duck in a
gold dress, hair ribbon and
sneakers.

Mid-January

Merimbula   New South Wales

Marlon and I were in Merimbula on the south-east coast. Each
day I marked online assignments and sorted out stuff for
Dad's estate but was fantastic to see pelicans, smell the salty
air, swim in icy-cold surf, and have no housework. Everything

that left the suitcase ended up on the floor or on the couch and stayed there. Nothing got hung up or put in drawers. Two days in, the unit was a write-off. We lived like we were on the run.

Yesterday Marlon leapt off
the couch and flew out of the
room after hearing the sound
of a huge beetle near his head.
Last night I saw it when I was
reading in bed and bolted out
of the room too. It was jet
black and the size of a golf ball.
Like a bumble bee, its wings
seem too small to keep it up.

*

What a day – four calls to the
bank, two emails to real estate
agent, three to settlement
agent and I'm marking. Top
fucking holiday. Can't wait for
the estate to be debt-free.

*

We can't see the beetle but
we know it's here. Hiding.
Polishing its pincers. When it
flew towards me, I cried out,
'No. No', in the way I imagine I
would if someone was coming
at me with an axe.

*

> Had a morning swim at the
> surf beach. Checked out a
> seal with Marlon and now he's
> in the pool with some kids.
> Marlon, that is.

The seal had been there for years. Lived alone under a bridge in the Merimbula Lake. Last summer a dugong from Queensland was stranded in the lake. It got caught in the East Australian Current and taken thousands of miles off course. Its condition deteriorated – the water was too cold and there wasn't enough sea-grass. The dugong was caught, given a police escort over the bridge to the airport and flown back to Queensland in a RAAF Hercules transporter. A crowd of us gathered to watch the plane take off. I often thought of the seal during that rescue. He was a long way from home too. I imagined him, out of his mind with jealousy at all the attention the dugong received, getting around balancing a ball on his nose, doing triple pikes, fucking up the last one as he turned to see who's watching. I'll tell you who was watching. No one.

> I'll call later. I have to drive
> around to find somewhere to
> print out some forms to sign
> and scan to send back to the
> settlement agent.

Marlon and I walked into town for Mexican. People on the bridge were staring at the seal but talking about the rescue of the dugong. Keep that up and the last we'll see of the seal will be him driving over the bridge with one flipper on the horn and the other giving us the finger.

> Grateful the real estate agent
> isn't a time waster. Gets back

to me fast. I need to know
things are moving.

First house sold. Casa Blanca. And the title of the Blandford
block was in Dad's name after 27 years. I was elated to have
one sale behind me.

Glorious to walk carrying
nothing except a few extra
Christmas kilos.

*

Pelicans land on the lake with
the steadiness and precision of
a jumbo coming in.

*

Mum and Tim arrived
yesterday. Everyone is relaxed.
Mum and Marlon are in the
pool. Mum sprightly as ever.
Tim reading on the couch. I'm
heading to the surf beach
before the afternoon winds
come up. Late yesterday
Tim and I went along the
boardwalk. Far enough to see
tiny crabs crawl out of the mud,
amongst the mangrove roots
during low tide. Tim tires easily
this summer.

*

Coastal winds throwing
everything around – sand,
beach equipment, birds. Saw a
seagull get flung across the sky
and then make a sudden turn
and gain control as if catching
itself from tripping.

*

Tim and I went to get some
oysters south of Pambula.
Oh my God what is it about
estuaries that I love.

*

I signed the contract to sell the corrugated-iron house. Settlement end of March. Two down.

*

One morning, after a swim, I got a call from L at the bank. If we sold the duplex for what the bank considered its market price, the bank would clear the debt. The remaining money would be wiped.

'You've let us know how you feel about the lending,' L said, 'and while we don't think there is any wrongdoing, we understand how much duress you have been under.'

I got off the phone and cried. The first person, in 11 months of dealing with that bank, to acknowledge how hard it was as the executor.

*

On the 25th of January I decided to keep a record of the correspondence for the estate as it was getting hectic and too complicated to keep track of all that was going on. The record of the next three months of correspondence was 16 pages of dot points.

*

The sale of Casa Blanca was in jeopardy. The bank was not releasing the title. It was supposed to be released a week earlier. The buyers were getting restless with the shifting settlement dates. After a day of seven calls, I found out I was 'unwilling' to sign a new agreement with the overdraft in the estate's name. An agreement I knew nothing about.

Apparently, I had requested a $200,000 reduction in the overdraft. I hadn't requested any reduction. I had asked for the money from the sale of Casa Blanca to go into the overdraft to reduce the amount of bank interest being charged. Thousands a month.

Another bank department – something to do with small businesses – was involved. I didn't even know the department existed. The confusion seemed to start when I wanted to put the sale money into the overdraft and the bank wanted it to pay off the mortgage debt. The mortgage loan was set up years ago as a small business loan. No one had told me that the bank's expectation was to put the money of the sale on the mortgage loan first.

*

For 11 months no-one explained anything despite my endless questions asking for clarity on the situation with the overdraft and the loan, and their promised return calls.

> Anguish. There's another word
> for the bank.

anguish ... *noun* severe mental distress or torture. *verb* (**anguishes, anguished, anguishing**) *tr & intr* to suffer or cause to suffer severe mental distress or torture. (ETYMOLOGY) 13c: from Latin *angustia* tightness.[2]

> I think the Small Business
> department is the one that
> kept lending Dad the money
> – the money borrowed to pay
> back the previous loan which
> was borrowed to pay back the
> previous loan which paid back
> the loan before that and so
> it goes back until you are out
> there wandering in the desert.

Two calls later I was told the money from the sale was going on the mortgage loan, not the overdraft. Once the second property – the duplex – was sold, the money would go on the overdraft then it would become unsecured. That's when I was

---

2 Chambers. (1999) Anguish. In *Chambers 21st century dictionary.* (p. 47).

told the bank wouldn't go after the deceased estate if there's a shortfall. I contacted the real estate agent to tell him to drop the price on the duplex. The bank and I wanted a quick sale.

Today I have made seven
calls and sent six emails to
Landgate, two banks, the
lawyers, the real estate agent
and the settlement agent,
regarding a lost title for the
corrugated-iron house that
I had signed the contract
for its sale in March. A lost
title application hadn't been
lodged. Christ. We can't have
a hold up on this sale too.

*

Did you hear the Kia's
representative Mr Cho's speech
to congratulate Federer on his
Australian Open win? You'll
never hear a finer speech. Full
of enthusiasm. Heartfelt. You
can only feel better for hearing
it.

*

I asked the person in the
bank in WA to just let me sell
the house and we can sort
out where the money goes
the week the money comes

through. She said that it
doesn't work that way.

Melbourne

I wrote an email to the person who informed me that I was
unwilling to sign the new agreement to say that the deceased
estate has already taken on Dad's debt; hence all the rental
income has been going into the overdraft since his death,
instead of paying other creditors:

> I had no idea until I spoke to you now, that I had to sign a
> new agreement. I am anxious we will lose the sale. Every
> phone call I get told different things.

I got a reply that the request had been escalated and there was
a request for some clear instructions on the next steps for this
to proceed.

I got up at 3 am and wrote an email to the same person:

Dear W,

> I was thinking about all this last night.
>
> The bank has happily charged fees and interest on
> my father's overdraft and loan since his death. Tens
> of thousands. No one in the bank has discussed any of
> this with me. I could not find one person who could talk
> to me about the situation, make a decision, answer my
> questions or alleviate some of the stress. I was promised
> calls back but never got them.

I understand that the bank is in the business of creating wealth for its shareholders but, so far, the bank's actions and its failure to let me know its processes and expectations has caused intolerable stress.

It took six months to get probate before I could put the properties on the market, and then, this long – another six months – to sell a property because of the financial downturn in Karratha.

No one at the bank except for L, this month, has acknowledged the duress that this has put me under.

Every other phone call to the bank is like trying to turn a rhino around, unaided.

All the rental income has gone into the overdraft. I have spent nearly $20,000 of my own money to manage the estate and to cover costs, including marketing costs to sell the properties and to stop legal action from creditors.

Now, a sale is in jeopardy because of this delay.

Who will cover the costs of putting the property back on the market if that's the case?

Why was it never mentioned to me that the sales of the two properties secured against the mortgage and overdraft meant I had to sign a new agreement?

I am tempted to go to the Ombudsman about not being told until yesterday about the new agreement/arrangement that apparently needs to be written and signed before the title is released. This is a failure of 'process'.

My father was a private man. He was a proud man. If he had told me his financial situation, he would never have been in this terrible position. I would never have let a retired 77-year-old man, who spent 42 years on hot tin roofs in the Pilbara, allow himself to be set up to lose everything.

Five hours later:

I got an email to say the bank approved the release of property with dollar-for-dollar reduction from net proceeds to be applied to permanent debt reduction of the overdraft.

> Adios Casa Blanca. They let me
> put the money on the overdraft
> and after the sale of the duplex,
> for anything over their valued
> price, they will wipe the rest
> of the debt. Dear God, what I
> have gone through for this.

> For a clean slate.

The next day I walked past a Vietnamese massage joint up the street and stopped – $20 for a 20-minute neck massage. My neck was killing me. I walked in and tapped the bell on the front counter. A girl came out from behind a curtain picking her teeth with a toothpick. Possibly Spam as that's what was on the front counter next to the ceramic waving cat – cans of Spam.

I undressed and got on the massage table. I was surprised to see directly below, through the head hole of the table, a white bin of dirty old crunched-up tissues. Jesus, what's gone on here? It's a bit much having to look at that. But, before long, the massage took my mind off those thoughts. The pressure on the knots was hard and painful. The relief was enormous. I should charge the fucking bank – they gave me the neck ache.

I got dressed. I put my glasses on. As I was leaving, I saw it wasn't a bin of dirty tissues. It was a white china plate of white plastic roses.

February

> I've lowered the price on the
> duplex. The bank wants a quick
> sale. Then, fingers crossed,
> that sale will be the end of it.
> They want a resolution too.

The title of the deeds to Dad's house came through. I, as executor of his estate, held the title. Cried.

> Just blew my photocopy
> funding budget for 2017 on the
> work photocopier.

After I had been on the phone all day to Western Australia, a letter arrived from the coroner in Port Hedland. They wanted to let me know that they couldn't establish the cause of 'my brother's death', so his death remained 'unascertainable'.

> Marlon and I had an apple
> each for dinner. Combination
> of my tiredness after half a
> bottle of beer and his refusal to
> eat anything from the fridge or
> cupboard.

I started the process of resealing the grant of probate in New South Wales. Registered the online probate notice. I had nearly completed the paperwork to send to the state's Supreme Court. I found a fantastic government website: 'What to do when a loved one dies'. Wish I'd known about it earlier. I completed what it outlined but I had done everything the long way around.

*

Back at work, another audit landed in our inbox. Out of the blue but 'must be completed before your class plans'. I had to read these forms over and over. There's a love of stringing three abstract nouns together to form incomprehensible headings:
Competency Matrix Outcomes
Performance Criteria Evidence
Core Initiative Deliverables

I can't hold these words together in my head. I read one word and as I read the next one, the previous one has slipped away. All thought slips away. Every year I continue to be baffled on how to map 'professional development activities' to 'units of competencies'.

> On the walk home, fruit bats
> flew over, heading south. One
> peeled off and disappeared,
> face first, into a fig tree across
> the road. A fig tree full of
> unripe fruit.

*

Yesterday I took Remy for a
walk and cut my nails at the
same time. I'd walk and shave
my legs if I could.

*

Terry rang to say Dad's house
is secure. He said he sensed
the orb spider was close as he
was unlocking the door. Then
he looked around and there
she was, dangling over the
meter box, next to the front
door, watching him.

We have to relocate her when
the house sells.

I love hearing she's ok. Terry
said his family has a similar
spider at home that wraps
prey and makes daisy chains of
beetles, insects and moths.

*

Got an offer on the duplex
today. Anniversary of Dad's
death so we're accepting it.

*

I'm still dealing with Karratha
stuff – waiting for calls

back from settlement agent,
regarding bank and the sale
of the second house and from
the real estate agent and an
electrician.

When I called the electrician, I said, 'I heard you knew Dad.'
'I did indeed,' he said. 'He was a good man. What can I do for
you?'
My voice caught. I told him it was just past the anniversary of
his death and there's been a lot to deal with over the year.
He said, 'I'm sure there would've been.'
I cried. He waited patiently for me to stop.

*

Lights lined up in the tunnel as we straightened up for the
home stretch to clear Dad's debts but nothing about the property sales was straightforward.

Chapter 17
Up in the air

March–June 2017   Melbourne

The two sales – the duplex and the corrugated-iron house – were in process but everything was up in the air. The sales often felt in jeopardy. Titles still hadn't been issued. The tyranny of distance was never more evident. I was still waiting for the replacement of the lost title of the corrugated-iron house to be issued for its sale and for the original grant of probate to be posted from Perth. It's the last piece of paperwork I needed to reseal probate in New South Wales.

Dad grinning over a beer on the Rec Club's Facebook page had been replaced with an ad for the band, 'Rusty Boots Acoustic'. The Rec Club had moved on. Meanwhile for the estate, the toing and froing of emails and calls continued. Such overload. Documents going to wrong addresses, delays in signing papers, knots in bureaucratic red tape, untimely responses and unanswered requests.

> After one particularly
> frustrating set of emails,
> Marcus said to add, 'Please find

enclosed a letter from angry
brother in jail. Very angry.'

*

Cool change expected around
four. Can't wait. One of the
best things about Melbourne is
the cold front's instant drop in
temperature. Always welcome.
Always beautiful.

*

Sent the five signed
documents to finalise the
sale of the corrugated-iron
house back to the settlement
agent. A neighbour lets me
scan documents and get his
signature to witness mine
often at a moment's notice.
Generous.

*

Just waiting for the title for the
corrugated iron house to come
through.

Cool evening. Walking home.
A magpie warbling on top of a
pencil pine. Chest puffed out
as if waiting for a medal to be
pinned on it.

Hit a wall so decided to stay
home and have a Campari
and raisin toast for dinner.
Just added a banana to cover
another food group.

Around this time, our second lawyer had been replaced with a third. I can't recall how I found out. I was probably told although I just remember emails being sent on behalf of a different lawyer. I imagined the Legal Assistant's desk to be overloaded with paperwork like a desk in Kafka's novel, *The Castle*. A never-empty inbox. I wasn't a big client – Dad's estate was a mess but I was doing a lot of the work myself – so I could see how we weren't a priority.

*

The bank wanted this to be over but after 12 months of being stonewalled and left in the dark, I didn't trust that they would keep to their word. The paperwork just had to end up on someone else's desk to set off another chain of confusion. I felt uneasy. Having said that, thanks to L, I had someone to call. He was always helpful, patient, but sick of me. Fair enough, I was sick of me.

Kev, who lived out in Dad's industrial yard as the caretaker, rang to say that he wanted to buy the block, so how much?

'I'm coming up in June,' I said. 'When it's cooler, to sort all that out.'
'OH, COME ON.'
I smiled at the snappy tone and said, 'I can't come up in that heat.'
'OH, COME ON.'

Not 'come on' in a welcoming-come-on-up-jovial-you-can-do-it tone, more what-the-fuck-is-wrong-with-you tone. I loved it. I spent the rest of the day walking around the house, re-enacting the conversation to Remy the dog.

> I assured Kev I wasn't going
> to spring a sudden sale on
> him and kick him out of the
> yard. Maybe he's worried. The
> top right corner of the yard is
> his home.

*

> Morning. I couldn't answer
> your last question yesterday
> as was feeling terribly anxious
> and teary.
>
> Then Marcus cheered me up
> with a text about a delivery
> truck getting bogged and
> how he was caught out in
> torrential rain, shirtless,
> holding up his daks that
> needed a belt with one hand
> and throwing bricks under the
> truck tyres with the other.

My siblings and I do like to tell a story or re-enact a scene, even if it's at our own expense. We like to entertain ourselves and others. My siblings' take on situations and their observations can make me laugh days later – sometimes until I can't breathe.

I think we do it to lighten the load. Of course, Dad was always good material. We appreciated the Dad in each of our stories and enactments, whether they were from being with him beside his broken-down Valiant on the Nullarbor, in a pokey caravan in Paraburdoo, on a rollercoaster at the Gold Coast, under the lights at the Melbourne Cricket Ground (MCG) or in a pub in Edinburgh where Dad walked like he was stumbling over dead people.

> Yesterday was a planned day
> off but I had to sign forms
> to allow early occupancy
> because of delays with a sale
> settlement, sort out Dad's
> house insurance, ok a plumber
> to check out a leak in a unit
> and contact an electrician to
> see if he completed something
> in the house for the sale.

I wrote to Nanette in Karratha to give her an update on the state of things. We had an exchange of texts about banks. I told her how I felt dread that the bank was going to renege on the deal as it's not in writing. I also told her about a situation that I had with another bank. She replied that she too had had dealings with that bank and was on her sixth caseworker. She also wrote that a friend of hers took up the job as the bank manager of the branch up there. He lasted six weeks. He said working for that bank was like working for *Dad's Army*.

> The mouse is back. Marlon
> saw it poke its head out from
> under the fridge. He said
> their eyes met.

The mouse that came to stay.

*

This, you will not believe:

Today the third lawyer sent
a letter to the bank about a
matter that I had contacted
the bank about and the
process was already under way.
He wrote on my behalf as the
appointed Executor, as the wife
of Richard John Trevitt.
Never did I think I'd have to
write the sentence: I am not
my father's wife.

I spoke to a person in yet
another department of the
bank who had received the
email to let him know that
the late Richard John Trevitt
was not my husband. He was
young and empathetic. Like
L, he was good to deal with.
Thorough. Considerate. The
bank needs those two but do
they need the bank?

*

On the train I was forced to
clamber to my seat over two
big, suited 60 year olds with

briefcases who didn't move a
muscle. I sat down and looked
at the three men around me,
including those two. I nodded
and said,
'Boys.'
The man opposite chuckled. I
grinned back. The two I had
to climb over glared at me,
which only made it funnier. The
two of us kept looking at the
other two and couldn't get the
grins off our faces. Twenty
minutes later, I got off. As the
train pulled away, I looked at
the two men and then at my
comrade. I waved goodbye. He
waved and threw back his head
laughing.

*

On the phone to L. He's been
so helpful. Reassures me that
the bank will see the sale of
the duplex as the end of it.
Pretty sure he wants to see the
end of me.

I thought about Nanette having caseworkers in the bank. Until
I talked to L, I had never spoken to the same person twice. Half
the time on the phone to the bank was spent repeating the
same stuff over and over and over and over.

> Sorry, can't talk – in
> negotiations with the mouse.

The title came through. The corrugated-iron house was sold. The relief was immense. I could start to pay the estate's outstanding debts.

> Home from errands –
> Officeworks and post office.
> Lodged forms for resealing of
> probate in NSW.

Dad's two small vacant blocks in rural New South Wales needed to go into my name so I could sell one and transfer the other to one of my brothers.

> Karratha police called to say
> they had Dad's toothbrush,
> hairbrush and driver's licence.
> I told them to destroy them. I
> was too shocked to think or to
> ask any questions.

*

> Don't know where the title
> is for the block Justin wants.
> Wasn't at Dad's and not with
> the bank. I'll apply for a
> replacement one.

> Losing titles or perhaps simply
> not thinking about where
> they might be means one day
> someone else has to.

April

I rang the Land Title Office in Sydney as I wanted to know how to get the titles of the two blocks in my name. I got on to a fast-talking bloke. He kept saying things like, 'What did I just say to you? ... Which form did I just tell you? ... Are you listening? ... Did I say open that file?'

'Hey. Slow down,' I said. 'How do you deal with someone who can't follow your instructions?'
'Tell them, they can't do it without a solicitor.'
I ended up telling him how Dad put everything into property in Karratha.
'I'm sorry your father passed away,' he said, 'but who invests everything in property in one place?'
He said he'd heard of a young woman who had 20 properties in a mining town and couldn't sell a thing.

*

I paid some of Dad's bills and calculated we have paid about $75,000 in debts for the year. This showed how much Dad had been losing and that excluded his living expenses and bank interest, and still they kept lending. Unconscionable.

Yet another word to define for the bank.

unconscionable ... *adj* **1** said of a person, behaviour, etc: without conscience; unscrupulous. **2** outrageous; unthinkable. **3** unreasonably excessive. **unconscionably** adverb. (ETYMOLOGY) 16c.[3]

---

3   Chambers. (1999) Unconscionable. In *Chambers 21st century dictionary.* (p. 1536).

*

I had to go back in June, as the mechanic wanted to leave Dad's industrial yard in July. I guess that's why Kev (the caretaker) rang me asking for the selling price of the yard. Dad's house needed to be sold too. It cost us around $10,000 a year to keep empty – land tax, rates, maintenance and insurance. The agent said it's the most original house he's had on his books.

The resealing of grant of probate in New South Wales came through. Two weeks after lodgement.

> At the footy – St Kilda and
> Collingwood. Bloke next to me
> reliving Collingwood's loss to
> St Kilda in 1966. We've gone
> through the last five moves
> before the losing goal, twice.
> Reckon I'll hear it again before
> the end but not before we
> relive Collingwood's 1964 loss
> against Melbourne.

*

In 2015, Marlon and I rugged Dad up in a St Kilda scarf and a borrowed jacket and took him to an AFL game at the Melbourne Cricket Ground (MCG). He had come over east to his 60th school reunion in Armidale and was visiting us on the way home. We sat high in the grandstand.

'They won't believe this when I tell them back at the Rec Club.'

Yet what really grabbed and held his attention and lit up his face until the final siren were the seagulls wheeling in at dusk when the stadium lights came on.

*

Sixteen days after a friend hand-delivered the paperwork for the transmission of the two blocks at Land and Property Information in Sydney, I had the titles in my name.

The sale of the duplex in Karratha was settled. That was the end of dealing with the bank yet it felt hard to believe it was really over.

> I took Remy for a long
> walk around the streets
> of Caulfield where you
> step back in time to the
> 1960s. Modernist houses in
> mint condition. Flat roofs,
> patterned brickwork, clean,
> horizontal lines, subtle motifs
> and corner windows.

*

> I'm 54 and want to design
> dollshouses. I'd be sad
> for the person who wrote
> that if I read that sentence
> anywhere.

May

I'm lying in my bed thinking
I need to get cracking on my
life. Why didn't I start in my
20s. So many years wasted
on unproductive thoughts
and shit jobs.

Hardly ... smithing away at
the soul and the meaning
of things, fate, free-will,
love.

Well, thanks, that puts a new
spin on things.

*

Marlon read my short story,
'Twenty Dollars.'
He said, to be honest, I don't
really like your stories.
Why?
No fists were made.

I laughed and thought that's
a good line. I'll have to
add that line to something
I write sometime. Then I
remembered a scene from
my short story, 'The Sun and
The Moon are Out':

I took the kids outside. Paulie walked out and lit up. Something hit the other side of the paling fence. It shook. Scuffling went on under the bushes next door.

'What's going on?' said Paulie.
'Blackbirds,' I said.
'Come on, you fuckin' bastard, come on,' said the neighbour.
'You'd think the bird had fists,' Paulie said.
I smiled and imagined it entering the ring as a six-foot, gloved-up contender. The fence got another blow.
'The neighbour's no featherweight,' I said.

Marlon can stop me in my
tracks like his dad could with
a deep and compassionate
observation when I hadn't
thought he was paying
attention.

He can make me pull my
head in.

*

Know what tips me over the
edge – modem going down and
trying to call Optus. I found a
card: Any faults or problems
with modem, ring this number.
After 3:41 minutes of pressing
numbers, I thought, now I'll
talk to someone. No siree.
Instead, I got an automated
voice sounding like a hyped-up,
half-hysterical radio announcer,

saying, 'Would you like to
download this sheet with how
to install your modem or would
you like to hang up?'

As if either option was a
thrilling prize for the customer.

Hours later and still feel my
blood vessels straining.

*

Watching Louis Theroux's show
on swingers. Little is more
off-putting than a swinging
baby-boomer. There's a
long-suffering, bone-tired wife
with saggy breasts that look
like socks with a bit of sand in
the bottom, walking around in
nothing but an apron, serving
finger food to paunchy naked
men including her husband
who's in the jacuzzi with
another woman. You've got to
see Louis's face as he looks
into the pool water.

*

Put an orange chenille
bedspread through my wash,
now staring at a clothes horse
of yellow clothes.

*

The reason I'm texting is I
was researching the history of
comedy and found the reason
why you love the M&M ad when
the M&M says, 'Why don't *you*
get in the bowl.' It has its roots
in commedia dell'arte – Italian
renaissance comedy. There is a
gag between stock characters
from those times. The Captain
asks Coviello (wily servant)
to do something difficult, like
capture a robber in the dark or
enter a cave. Coviello replies,
'Why don't *you* get in the cave?'
Your M&Ms are wily servants.

*

In class I did, I have to say,
an impressive impersonation
of the mother of a boy from
primary school who saw
me shout at the automated
voice coming out of a Coles
self-serve machine. She
stood directly in front of me
but pretended she hadn't
seen me.
Small class today. Students
arrived without their scripts
to work on, so we had to do
something else.

Scene: A supermarket aisle.
Character does something
foolish and is forced to
confront someone they didn't
want to see ...
What's at stake for your
character? Include oranges.
Twenty minutes.

*

Did you watch the game last
night? I thought that was like
a finals game. Moments later,
Matthew Richardson (Richo)[4]
said the same thing. Some of
my friends say he states the
obvious. He does. Perfectly.
I love Richo.

My favourite line of Richo's
was from years ago when he
interviewed the captain of a
team that had just won the AFL
grand final,
'What does it feel like,' he
said and as he moved the mic
across in front of the captain,
he said softly, 'I never played a
grand final.'

*

---

4 Matthew Richardson is a former Australian Rules footballer who played for
Richmond. He is now a media commentator for telecast matches.

On the train thinking of a
friend's 61,316 unread emails
and remembering the time
when every single email felt
important.

I told a man in a suit on the
train about the 61,000 unread
emails and he said that his
unread emails sit between
400,000–600,000.

*

Marlon (14) came home from
footy with some corkies he
reckons were done by 'men' on
the field.

*

Last night Marlon told me that
some boys in his Year 9 were
given condoms in their Health
class. He said you should see
how many ripped wrappers are
in the school yard. He reckons
no condoms went home
because the boys were making
balloons or wearing them over
their shoes.
I adore this age group.

He reckons I should teach in a
high school. Not his, of course.

*

A council man from Karratha
contacted me. The grass at
Dad's place is knee high and
the neighbours are worried
about snakes. He said for
me to try to find someone to
slash it and not mention I'm in
Melbourne.

*

Booked Marlon on a school trip
to go snowboarding. So happy
he has something to look
forward to.

I was between classes when the lawyer sent an email to say
the bank sent them a bank statement to say we still owed on
the loan. I went outside to walk off a sick-to-the-stomach
feeling. L wasn't at his desk. I was so thrown, the streetscape
felt altered, almost unrecognisable. I had to go back to class. I
couldn't call the bank until the next day.

*

I got home that evening and opened the coroner's third and
final letter. They were unable to ascertain the cause of death
and concluded our father, Richard John Trevitt, died of
natural causes.

*

I rang the bank first thing in the morning. All finalised. I went to the local branch to make sure. The account was closed. Dad's debt had been cleared.

I'm staring out into my overgrown backyard, feeling like a fucking General. Where's the roar from my troops?

*

In a change room watching myself go from a full General to a woman in her 50s who really should buy a home treadmill.

That's why change rooms are called change rooms – you're guaranteed a change of mood every time you leave one.

*

Now I know why William Shatner wanted to be called Captain off set.

Chapter 18
Misconduct is rife

June 2017   Melbourne

Dad had trusted the bank in the same way he would have trusted a bank in the 1970s. A time when the bank manager would have formed a relationship of integrity with the customers. After Dad had shot through and Mum found the letter to say we had lost everything and had to be out of the house within the month, she went to the bank. The branch manager worked with her. He let us stay in the house until the end of the second school term, to lessen the disruption to our schooling. He gave my mother time to absorb the unravelling of our lives before we had to move. He let us keep the family furniture.

He understood. He showed compassion. He gave a shit. The banking world changed without Dad in tow. It turned into a deregulated corporate industry with a culture of greed from the top down and a bureaucratic system that no longer acted on empathy. A system that appeals to the worst in people. Misconduct was rife. Unethical lending practices went unchecked, and customers were blatantly disregarded. This combined with the mining bust, Dad's age, and his profound, possibly pathological difficulty in letting go of anything dug him a hole from which he couldn't escape.

The overdraft had been unsustainable for years. Anyone could have seen the properties were his super and retirement fund.

> Heading back to Karratha
> with Marcus to clean up the
> two units, Dad's house and
> the industrial yard and set up
> the final sales. Ok now until
> something goes wrong. Little in
> reserve.

*

> An email went out from a
> manager at work telling us all
> to tidy up our work desks as a
> band of managers was coming
> through on a 'leadership walk'.
> We looked at our desks, at
> each other, laughed and went
> home.

*

> *For A Few Dollars More* is
> on TV. Clint's after a posse
> of bandits in the desert. A
> shoot-out in my living room
> while organising paperwork.
> Can't ask for much more.

*

I cleaned the house. What is
it with vacuuming? You feel
lighter and the size of your
place doubles.

*

My heart is ripped out of my
chest. The bloke who mowed
Dad's front yard killed the orb
spider. My fault. I thought, Oh
my God he'll do a big clean
up – the eaves – I have to let
him know to leave the orb, but
I was too late.

*

Marcus and I fly out tomorrow.
Final trip over there.

Chapter 19
The chisel

Late June 2017 Karratha

At Melbourne's Tullamarine Airport, Marcus had screwed up his boarding pass thinking it was rubbish. Once it was sorted, we passed through the metal scanner. Marcus was stopped. He had to get a pouch to send through to Karratha with our other bags, as he tried to take a chisel in his carry-on bag for the cabin. The security man inspecting the bags studied the chisel. He turned it around gently in his hand and said, 'This is beautiful.'

We arrived in Karratha late in the afternoon. Nanette picked us up from the airport. Dad's units were empty. We stayed in one as it was easier to be in than Dad's house. I persuaded Marcus to come to the Rec Club. A rugby league game was on the big screen. He follows rugby league and AFL. He follows many sports. Few people understand sport psychology like Marcus. He has been watching and analysing rugby league players and their teams since his teenage years in the '70s.

*

In 2015, Marcus entered the New South Wales public National Rugby League (NRL) tipping competition. There were 76,404 tipsters. On the last day of the competition, Round 26, three games to go, 240 minutes of football, the risk-taker Hilly79 in third place, in second place, Joker, and, in first place, with a game up, was Marco Magnifico – my brother, Marcus.

After a harrowing day of upsets, where I hadn't felt my hands all day and Marcus thought the beating of his heart was music coming from a neighbour's house, and with one game left, Marcus was still in the lead. He could 'feel the cool breeze out in front.'

But would Hilly make his break now? Marcus had minutes to calculate the margins that he needed to beat Hilly if Hilly backed the underdog. He knew Hilly's form. He knew Hilly was brave.

The siren for the last game sounded. I waited. Marcus couldn't call out on his landline and he had lost his mobile phone. A few minutes later, I got an email:

'Warriors have scored. Not good. What did the other boys pick as a margin? What?'

Sportsbet hadn't updated the tipsters' board.

I waited. And waited.

Five minutes later, he sent another email:

'Game over. They (Joker and Hilly79) marched with Marco Magnifico.'

My heart spiked before I understood it.

He won. Marcus had won. Exhilarating. He won $100,000 yet hadn't seen a game all season. He didn't own a TV.

Earlier that day, I had called Dad to wish him happy Father's Day. I didn't tell him about Marcus as Marcus didn't want to feel the pressure of others' expectations. Dad and I talked weather. We compared temperatures – a favourite topic where we didn't have to think.

'I had to put on two tee-shirts, but still in shorts and thongs,' he said.
'I'm inside in a puffer jacket, scarf and boots.'

Even after 30 years, the difference always seemed to surprise us. He talked about the AFL footy competition at the Rec Club. He was coming second or third.

'How many in the comp?'
'A lot, 70.'

70. 70? Try 76,404, I wanted to shout and felt instantly ill with apprehension.

*

When Marcus and I walked into the Rec Club, J, the pool player, was clowning around and entertaining his friend. He hadn't seen us. He approached the bar as we signed in. I said, 'Hello.' I've never seen someone look so spooked. He bought two drinks and went back to his table. I imagined turning around to see a hole in the wall in the shape of a fleeing man who's just been shot in the back.

He played a game of pool, went out for a cigarette, came back in, played another game or two, maybe another drink, and left with his friend. We didn't make eye contact after the initial hello. It was disappointing to see him leave. I would have loved to have resolved whatever it was with us, to put our minds at rest, but I hadn't approached him either.

Despite that, it was good to be out.

> Quiet at Rec Club. Still the
> finest jukebox. Watched a good
> game of footy on the screen
> and played pool with Marcus.

*

> Six am here – the time
> difference means we wake
> early. I'm at the cemetery to
> say hello to Dad and tell him
> why we're here but mostly to
> tell him he's debt-free.
> Feeling heavy hearted. Poor
> Dad – that was probably all he
> had wanted to hear for years.

Marcus and I hit the ground running. In the first few days, we checked out the units and Dad's place, and drove out to the industrial yard. I had to visit the real estate agent, the council and the accountant and do some cleaning. Marcus started clearing and repairing. As well as a unit to rent out or sell – we were undecided at the time – and Dad's place to sell, I needed to set up the sale of Dad's industrial yard as the mechanic was moving out the following month to a place with a bigger shed. This meant that Kev the caretaker had to go too.

Oh, to see the empty space in
the carport where the golden
orb had her web. Awful. Dad
would have loved her too.

*

Dad's house has a good aspect
and established gum trees
but needs a shit load of work
that requires thousands-upon-
thousands to make liveable.

*

Marcus is thinking of living up
here.

*

Roebourne Races tomorrow.
We're going. Can't wait.

We arrived at the races as the track was being watered. Not as
many people as I had expected. The big race, the Roebourne
Cup, was coming up in July. Dad had put the roof on the Nor
West Jockey Club. I kept wanting someone to mention the
club or the roof so I could say, 'Yeah, our dad did that.' Maybe
really to say, 'Hey we're a part of all this too.'

Put money on a horse called Steve. Something else to see the
horses run in red dirt against the huge expanse of blue. By the
time they turned in to the home straight, the horses out the
back were hidden in the red dust. By the time they crossed the
finish line so were the spectators.

Steve won.

That's it – I'm just backing
horses with boys' first names.

*

Early evening. Watching
local Aussie Rules game on
oval near Dad's. Top Pilbara
league. Karratha Falcons
v Port Hedland Rovers.
Glorious breeze. Fast game.
At times bullet fast. Noisy.
Lots of twists and turns and
side-stepping and shouting.
Low and accurate kicks on
the run. Fantastic.

*

Out Saturday night. Had
fun playing pool with one of
Dad's friends and then, when
he left, with anyone who
wanted a game. Quiet. Ran
the jukebox for five hours.
I wouldn't let anyone else
near it. Blokes kept giving
me coins. Some were pretty
pissed and bleary eyed,
probably thought they were
giving coins to, and chatting
to, a set of identical twins.

My brother and I worked on different things. We are independent and like to make our own decisions. We have distinctive approaches and ways of doing things. We use time differently. I had a strict timeframe of nine days in which to complete what I needed to complete. I had to keep things moving. I had to use lists. Marcus was staying on so he did the repairs at his own pace. He often worked on a few things at once whereas I liked to finish something before starting on another project.

*

Dad's friend, a builder, did a walk-through of Dad's house with us and quickly itemised what needed to be done for us – $40,000 – and that wasn't including labour. That was for basic changes. I wasn't going to pour money into the house from afar. It would be like a broken beer tap that no one could turn off. Dad hadn't spent a cent on the place for years and didn't request that I do so in the will.

> Marcus has cleared up heaps.
> He works for days until he's
> done in and then rests like
> a cat.

*

> Big day of negotiating
> everything with everyone.
> It's 24/7. Wiped out.

*

Marcus won't be living here. He
has decided he can't cope with
the heat.

New moon. I love the country
here but the heat is something
to contend with. Like facing a
relentless bully who is never
going away.

Dad's place. God. Despairing. All I felt in it was his isolation.
An extension of his neglect that went back decades. And to be
there without the orb spider.

Dad's neighbour, S, had moved out too. I missed his morning
greetings.

I met with a real estate
agent about the value of the
industrial block. I had to tell
the caretaker we want more
than he offered.

Unexpected call from a bloke
who leased a yard in the same
street as Dad's yard. He owns
flatbed trucks. A big possibility
he wants, and can afford, the
block. If he takes it, Kev can
stay there. He buys the block
he buys Kev.

Marcus and I waited for nearly 45 minutes for an Indian
dinner. We watched families who came in after us get their
food. We got dizzy with hunger. I got floppy with laughter at

Marcus's gags. That was after I had read a review under the heading: '2 Hours'. A table of customers had claimed they waited two hours. They said they were ignored. The restaurant replied, 'How could we ignore you – you were yelling at the manager all night.' And then the restaurant wrote they found the receipt and the time that the customers had arrived and it wasn't two hours, so could they change their heading to '1 hour 10 minutes'.

*

We decided to rent the unit. The real estate agent said units aren't selling. We decided to wait in the hope the prices lift.

> Got savvy young woman from
> the real estate to tell us what
> we need to do for the unit to
> be rentable. She was smart,
> clear-headed and practical.
> She should run her own
> show. She's tough. Moved to
> Karratha. Raising her son on
> her own. She wore a heavy
> suit of armour. I want to plead
> with her – please don't. I wore
> a suit like that for years. Don't,
> it's not fun. You're great, feel
> all you feel.

*

> At the cemetery giving Dad an
> update.

*

Marcus has decided he'd like
one of the units.

*

Met Dad's accountant. I took
pages of notes. A mess of
scribbles that only I can read
of what she needs from me to
complete a tax return for the
estate. Daunting.

*

This afternoon I ran into a
woman from the Rec club, in
Coles, who I like a lot – funny,
warm, ratbaggy – and she
invited me to watch the
women's darts at the Rec Club.

*

At Club. Running the jukebox
and watching the women play
darts. My God, they can play.
The accuracy. The precision.
The lightness of the throw.

After the dart games were over,
I went out to the beer garden
and sat with some women I
didn't know. Friendly.

The women were my age. They talked about how much they loved the Hungry Jack's Whopper. One had a story of how her friend bought her a Whopper at Perth airport to bring back to Karratha and how she nearly went out of her mind when the flight was delayed a few hours and she didn't get her burger until 10:30 pm. Another had a similar story of her family sitting up waiting for their Whoppers to fly in. Another woman put her Whopper in the fridge for later and one of her kids ate it.

Bet she will think of that burger her kid ate from time to time. In 1983, when I was 19, my housemate made a batch of perfect golden potato chips. During dinner I had to take a call on the landline in another room. I had saved the best chip till last and decided to have it after the call. I returned to the kitchen to find my plate had been cleared. The chip was in the bin. I still think of that chip.

The women in the beer garden told me you can take a bucket of KFC to Port Hedland two hours away, put it on Facebook's Buy Swap Port Hedland on your way into town and you'll pay for your trip up and back.

That night a woman said, after finding out I was the Prof's daughter, 'Oh. You have his expressions.' Maybe that's what was depressing me – let down my guard and Dad emerges. This time, a lot of blokes came up to me with stories about Dad. More so than any other time. It was like now they felt his absence.

> Haven't been able to drive into
> the country and see the hills
> and rocks and colours that
> can take me away from the

day-to-day grind of sorting out
the estate.

Friday night, I went to the Rec Club. Marcus didn't want to come. He didn't like being around a lot of drinking. I didn't either but I didn't want to sit in the unit staring at my phone and to go for a night walk felt unsafe. There weren't many people that night. Many had gone to Marble Bar – four and a half hours away – for the Marble Bar races and annual Undie Run.

N was there. He saw me and smiled warmly as if my last trip over there had never happened. I smiled back. I didn't know why the shift but I was relieved there was no animosity. I monopolised the jukebox. I had pockets full of other people's coins. When someone wanted to put a song on, I vetoed it. Either, 'Yep, go for it' or 'No, wait till next week when I'm not here.'

A few hours in, a bloke came over and introduced himself. E. A foreman. On my last trip, I had seen him in there, sitting on his own watching games of pool.

His delivery was dry, droll and direct. I found him amusing. After a short while, he said, 'I'm 40, is that all right?'
'Sorry?'
'You're 50, I'm 40, so why not?'
'Sorry?'
'The night is yours. We can do whatever you like. If you want to watch TV or have an ice-cream. Whatever you want ... What else you going to do?'

He had a point. I told him I'd think about it and went back to the jukebox. He had made me smile so it wasn't hard to think, 'Why not?'

Marcus sent a text message asking if I was ok.

> Running the jukebox.
> Everything's fine.

I never had more than two drinks when I was out in Karratha. I'm not a drinker but consciously or unconsciously I knew, regardless of Karratha being Dad's town, I was an outsider. Marcus felt that too. He was protective and I appreciated that.

I did anticipate a *Wake in Fright* welcome whenever I entered the Rec Club on my own. Only when I saw a familiar and friendly face did the tension fall away. Hard to know if the isolation and frontier aspect of the town triggered my apprehension or if it was from my need for a complete blast of freedom from being so responsible all the time, which kind of meant anything could happen.

Ironically, I reinvented myself up there, like Dad had in the '70s. The difference – I always had a plane ticket out of there.

I got back to the unit around dawn for Marcus's sake.

> Last night, at 10 pm, I'm
> in a Colorbond compound
> on a king-sized bed with a
> droll foreman who hadn't
> quite caught my name,
> his Rottweiler beside
> the bed playing with its
> soft, squeaky toys and a
> narky little Pomeranian
> wanting more bed space
> and 200 metres away,
> my brother is singing,

'supercalifragilisticexpialidoc
ious' to young Chinese
cleaners to help them speak
English.

E was easy to spend a night with. Generous. Welcoming.
Bright. Affectionate.

During the night he got
up to get some water. He
picked up his narky little
dog and, as he walked
out, threw her on the bed
and said, 'Meet your new
mother.'

He said he was shy. He may well be but he wasn't that night.
He talked a lot. I enjoyed the droll delivery. I liked the way he
talked about his family over east. I liked how he thought about
things. I liked the way he had dropped his guard.

In the afternoon, Marcus and I went for a drive to Point
Samson. My eyes hung out of my head. We saw yet another
fantastic iron-ore train pass by like something prehistoric
emerging out of the ground.

Seven pm. At the former
'Walkabout' – now a Sports
Bar. Marcus talking NRL to
a young bloke. Funny and
knowledgeable conversation
between them. Place is
empty as patrons are away
at the Marble Bar Cup.

Bed soon. Wrecked. Having
an early night. I leave
tomorrow. Marcus is staying
on to clear out Dad's place.

*

Leaving Dad's house for the
last time. Sad. Beautiful day
for a farewell.

Always loss. Today it's hard
not to feel its tremor in
everything. Dread driving
away.

*

Unit ready for tenancy.
Industrial site ready to be
sold. Neighbour out there
wants it. Fingers crossed
that he and I can strike a
deal otherwise I'll get the
real estate agent who rented
Dad's properties to sell it.

*

Just landed in Perth.
Emotional flight. Sat next
to a gorgeous 31-year-old
woman. So present. Amazing.

She was an angel. She was
with her beautiful baby boy.
Calm, adventurous and an
exquisite listener. A deep
pool. We had each other in
tears. We told each other
things we hadn't told anyone.
We asked each other intense
questions. We knew each
other was up for it. No
judgement, no repercussions.
Both of us loved it. She said
she was getting off the plane
feeling more-ish. Same.
The pure intimacy of
strangers.

*

Marcus texted to say he
wants Dad's house, and not
the unit.

Chapter 20
A cupcake fell from the sky

July 2017   **Melbourne**

My dealings with the bank were over but selling properties, thousands of miles away, in a town that had gone bust was, at best, time consuming and at worst, a nightmare. Life in Melbourne was compromised.

Marcus wanting Dad's house caused me great concern. I couldn't see how it was possible with an equal breakdown of the inheritance. Very hard to predict what that would be, as we had to sell when Pilbara property prices were rock bottom – properties across the region were selling for as little as a fifth of their value from four years earlier.

> At work, devising a semester
> of classes and assignments for
> a subject I have never taught.
> Have acres of marking.

*

> A cupcake fell out of the sky.
> Landed with a thud. Intact.

Lunchtime crowd on the street.
Tempted but I was spotted
having the thought.

*

Have you ever seen a bird fall
from the sky? Often surprised
by how few dead birds I see.

*

On the train home from
work. Kids on the train with
loud music. Kind of great. No
phones. Talking like they are at
a party.

I know one of the kids from
Marlon's primary school days.
Always liked her a lot. Open.
Friendly. Tough life. Always
thought it would have been
particularly hard for her in
such a middle-class school.
She gave a moving speech
at end of Year 6 about her
mum and how she was strong
and understood a lot about
things. Sincere. Her own words.
Memorable.

A friend of Dad's rang to ask if a friend of hers and Dad's, who
was ill, could rent one of Dad's units for $100. Marcus was
staying in one and we had someone lined up to rent the other

one short-term but even if we'd said 'ok', at that requested price, we would have had to cover the shortfall to cover the expenses of having the unit in Karratha. The friend then asked if he could live at Dad's. I had to say 'no'. I didn't feel good about it but the house was a dire place for anyone let alone someone who was sick. Dirty cement floor, no stove, no air-con, no furniture, windows that can't be locked, broken cupboards, leaking toilets, tree roots coming up through bathroom tiles and a shower I'd rather no-one saw.

Something told me Dad would have dealt with a lot of requests like that. Something told me Dad would have found saying 'no' hard, if not impossible. Dad had a stern manner but under it all, he was a soft touch. We knew he had lent tens of thousands over the years and a fair whack didn't come back. I didn't like to think about Dad, or anyone in my family, being taken for a ride. I'm sure many thought Dad died leaving a fortune.

> Marcus is still up there. He got
> a call too.

*

> Watching footy. I love Richo.
> His haircut is awful, all these
> military-neat haircuts make the
> men look like their brain cells
> have called it a day, so unsexy,
> but I love Richo. He has that
> big, open, guileless face and
> wears his big, open heart on
> his sleeve.
>
> I think people who bag him
> are being unkind. They miss

the point. They can't see the
openness, the sweetness, and
be thankful it's on mainstream
TV.

*

I'm losing my mind with
auditing forms at work. Who
wouldn't if you like plain and
purposeful language. Absolute
administrative overload. Like
all the teachers here, I just
want to work on class notes.

I had to move an OH&S poster with ugly cartoon characters telling us to report **Near Misses** away from my desk. **Who can look at the font Comic Sans all day and feel by the end that anything matters.**

Our office got into trouble for not reporting enough **Near Misses**. We were compared with another office on another campus that had reported many. My first thought was the full-time staff there had got together over microwaved noodles and made stuff up.

*

Fifteen texts and emails and
five calls to Karratha as well as
trying to juggle a truckload of
paperwork for the estate and
work.

*

My phone started to call itself
every minute. The only way
to stop my phone from calling
itself was to block it. My only
blocked number in the phone is
my own number.

*

I just ate a packet of biscuits.

I begged myself not to.

B e g g e d.

*

When's Steve racing next? I'm
putting my inheritance on him.
Double or nothing.

*

The new tenant in one of the
units is helping to fix up a
mining company's 100 houses
to sell. We have to sell before
those houses get on the
market.

I was trying to sell Dad's industrial site privately so it didn't
sit empty on the market for a year. I made a counter offer. The
bloke was approaching his bank. I wanted him to have it.

Have I become a wheeler
dealer? God, no. I'm not tough.
I'm clear-headed, logical and
observant and can hear tone
well on the phone, but not
tough. Selling makes me ill.

The potential buyer got back to me. Said it was too much.

Bryan came in. That's it – only
back horses with the first
name of a man. So far – Steve,
Terry, Bryan. I saw a Khan was
racing. Missed it.

*

I'll come to the footy with you.
I'm having a day off to work
out what to do about Dad's
yard. Having a day off to work
out what to do isn't a day off.

I am meeting M afterwards.
She wants to buy something
to wear for her son's wedding.
You've seen what's out there
in shops. I told her we're
approaching this like a military
operation. Foot soldiers. Into
a shop, walk around the racks
without breaking stride, and
out again.

A marching cadence: left, left,
left, right, left we can't possibly
wear that, left, left ...

Mid July

SOLD.

I did it. I sold the industrial yard. Took a swig of whisky and
rang him. I said, 'I want you to have it ... but for $10,000 more.'
Both of us were silent for what felt like minutes and then he
said, 'Right-o.' So pleased. He knew what he was getting. A
good-sized block and Kev.

> On train and some poor
> bastard is fighting Centrelink.
> He's pacing. His phone is
> tiny in his huge hand. He's
> talking but it's clear they
> aren't listening. He's pretty
> inarticulate and incoherent but
> if you listen you can get what
> he's saying. He's in despair.
> Desperate. He has been cut
> off and wants to know why. He
> doesn't have internet access.
> He's losing it. They will hang
> up on him soon.
>
> He got off the train saying
> into the phone, 'You need
> better communication skills,
> lady, if you're going to break

someone's heart and crush
their spir ... '

*

Remy and I got caught in hail.
We're in front of the heater,
drying off. This is one cold
winter.

*

Settlement for Dad's yard in
three weeks. First easy sale.
The mechanic moves out next
week. Kev stays.

*

Oh my God, I just passed a
man who looks EXACTLY like
Dad. Same nose, face, the way
his head sits on his shoulders.
Everything. My heart skipped
a beat.

I went back and spoke to him.
His surname is Trott.

*

A woman in her 80s gets off
the train in a summer hat with
two wobbly pink flowers on
long stems attached. Like a

cartoon flowerpot. She walks
past the Myki ticket stand
and stops. She looks at it as
if expecting something free to
pop out. She waits and then,
when nothing happens, she
walks on.

*

Marlon is having five boys over
tonight for a sleepover. They
are going into town to the
skate park.

I like how these boys play. Lots
of public transport. City is a
playground.

After some painful discussions, my brother realised that to
own Dad's place was impossible but he still wanted to paint
it with the person who had been Dad's painter for years. He
said the painter has helped him see what he didn't have to do,
mostly through facial expressions and lines like, 'Mate, what
are you talking about?'

He had talked of doing more to the place but without a clear
itemised budget and timeframe, the house would be a bottomless pit. I knew the crazy prices of materials and labour and
the costs to keep a house empty up there.

Tossed and turned all night and got four minutes' sleep.

August

At Marlon's footy in Brighton.
In score box. New computer
system but that's not the
excuse for delayed scores on
the scoreboard. The other
team's scorer and I missed a
goal while working out seating
for Remy off the cold concrete
floor. We looked up to see the
boys back in the middle.

Can always trust a parent
nearby to give you an
incredulous look.

Timekeeping is nerve wracking.
Feel like a clown as soon as I
sit down especially when the
incompetence is lit up on a
giant scoreboard.

*

Off to photocopy all the
documents for the sale of
Dad's yard and then onto the
post office. The new owner and
I have signed. Today feels like
a good day.

*

Remember the beautiful line
in *Out of Africa* about knowing
they walked a long way from
the Kikuyu Reserve to the
post office because there
was something heavy on
their hearts that they wanted
to communicate and what
they came back with was a
nonsensical letter.

What a book.

I had a farm in Africa.

I had a father in Karratha.

Chapter 21
Loggerheads

Marcus wanted to take on the renovations of Dad's for the estate. He had an idea he could fix it over two winters. The house would be unrentable for the duration. This put us at loggerheads for the first time. I didn't want to spend estate money on it especially without a workable itemised budget of materials, expenses and the labour costs. I worried that time and costs would spin out of control. It was an enormous job for one person. I needed to keep moving with the process of selling and finalising the estate. I needed this to be over for my son's sake and mine.

I was angry that Dad had left such a mess. A mess we had to clean up and that had caused friction between Marcus and me. Marcus didn't have to but he cared about it enough to feel compelled to renovate and repair Dad's place.

Dad had abandoned us but we never abandoned him. We accepted his choices and cared about his welfare when he was alive and then about his estate when he died.

Our lives carried the legacy of Dad's desertion but we never pushed him to face the life-long effect that loss of trust had upon us. Years ago, I had said to Dad he could be kinder to my brothers. He was hurt. He said, 'I have never been mean to anyone in my life.'

But unwittingly he had. After he walked out, he never looked at us and thought he needed to say an encouraging word or to apologise.

Instead, his stern, often gruff manner and his silence could be, and often was, interpreted as disapproval or, worse still, disappointment.

'It's not the Trevitt way,' he said.
'What?' I said. 'To encourage?'
'Yes, why, do you?'
'I'm a teacher, Dad, that's what I do: help students to take courage.'

*

Dad was unaware of his power over us. When we were growing up, he sometimes felt he had to assert his authority but I don't mean that, I mean, he was unaware of his power over our emotions, over our hearts.

*

In my 20s, during one of Dad's visits to Sydney, he said to me, 'You are an angry young woman.'

It wasn't an accusation for he was never the target nor was it something to discuss further and consider. It was simply an observation, and he was right. My anger mis-fired elsewhere, in all directions.

Mostly my rage was internal and connected to my struggles with relationships – to have them, to trust them and to get out of them. I was often equivocal about my relationships yet when they ended, I always felt the same. Desolate. I couldn't understand, and judged, my inability to get back on steady ground.

In my early 30s, I started to write short stories. Dad asked to read one. He took it into the kitchen of my St Kilda flat. I felt ill. The stories mattered to me and so did his opinion. Twenty minutes later he came back into the living room, bright-eyed.

'Oh Jeez,' he said. 'That was good.'
He looked up.
'It's like you've been out there in the wild with the cut-throats,' he said. 'But you've led such a sheltered life.'

Sheltered? I thought. Sheltered? You took my shelter from me when I was a kid. Of course, I didn't say this to him. He had taken the story seriously and that was enough.

However, the feeling of being stranded in the wild, every time a relationship went awry, continued into my 30s. It affected everyday life. I tried hard to hold things together. When I could, I pretended to be ok but I was in trouble and knew it. I went to a doctor and asked to see a psychiatrist.

The first time in his room he asked why I wanted to see him. I told him. I cried. He listened and took notes. After some time, he stopped writing.

'You sound in distress,' he said.

Maybe he said, 'terrible distress'. I can't remember. I do remember the effect of his words. Something cracked open in me and the release was enormous. I had never used the word 'distress' to describe how I felt. There was so much to take in. For the first time in I don't know how long, I sat feeling what I felt without any judgement, including my own.

*

One night, in the early months of seeing him, I dreamt I had come up through a manhole in the floor on to the deck of ship. There was a bar and a dance floor and a party in full swing – colour, music, swirling lights, laughter, frivolity. I looked around and thought, I can't do this. I dived back through the manhole into the darkness of the ship's hull. As I swam down, through the thick black water and tangle of oily ropes, I thought, I have to go deep. Really deep.

Chapter 22
Tax return

Late August–October 2017　　**Melbourne**

Paperwork for the estate's 2016–2017 tax return was spread across horizontal surfaces all over my house. It included the paperwork for the sales of the first three properties. The remaining unsold properties were soon to go on the market.

> On the train. Packed. A
> drug-addled bloke is standing
> and leaning over a couple who
> are sitting down. They are
> on their phones and haven't
> noticed he's blowing steam on
> the window above them and
> drawing love hearts in it. No
> one has noticed that he's in his
> own lovesick world.

The marking system of the online college was changing. Less work. Less money but I got time back. The writing course was being slowly phased out. Apparently, the course was too expensive to market.

Two girls on the sideline of
Marlon's footy game. Icy
cold morning – frost on the
ground – yet in thin tops and
jeans with big holes. Fake tans,
manicured, frozen and silent.
They left miserable and hunchy
with cold. Too much make-up.
So self-conscious. Pretty
smiles. What terrible pressure
they're under.

*

An online student who
completed our course sent me
an email to say she puts her
other teacher and me on top of
her 'pedal stool'.

*

Just left work. 9 am–6:30 pm.
No lunch break. Paid for 7.5
hours.

I have more and more students with difficulties that make
study almost impossible for them. Insecure housing, little
money, poorly managed stress, ineffective medication. Difficulties that the staff of whichever job provider they were with
would have seen and yet, still, put them in a demanding full-
time Certificate IV course. Hard to know how much control
some students had over the decision to do the course. And if
the students didn't get through it, where did that leave them?

I often wished for a more manageable, government-funded bridging course for these students. One that gave the students new skills and confidence and the opportunity to go on if they wanted to.

September

By September it became clear that I had to go back to Karratha once again before the heat set in and arrange for Dad's house to go on the market. Agony. Marcus and I were in a state over this. We had never clashed until now. He wanted to do it up and I needed to sell. The estate couldn't take on the unforeseen costs. It had rattled me so much I taught a class with a dress on inside out.

> At the footy ground, waiting
> for the first batch of bacon
> and egg rolls. Why do they
> always taste better here
> than at home?

> Marlon is getting faster on
> the footy field. Thank God
> he can accelerate like that.
> Half the 15 year olds are
> bearded men.

I was home late, often, from work. I was doing more and more unpaid counselling work to keep some students on an even keel.

> Paperwork for the estate's
> tax continues to spill all over
> in the house. On a mad roll.

Should have it finalised this
week. Weeks and weeks of
gathering all the information
and documents the accountant
needs.

Nerida's at her house working
on umpteen spreadsheets.

*

Watched Richmond win the
AFL Grand Final against
Adelaide for Richo's response.
Glorious unashamed tears for
Richmond's win. Overwhelmed.
I love Richo.

*

Fly to Karratha in a week.
First to Fremantle for a strata
meeting about the block where
we have two units and then
the next day on to Karratha. As
always, in school holidays.

October

Sorry can't meet up tonight
have to organize stuff for
Karratha trip. Booked three
nights in a motel with palm
trees and a pool and then I'll

stay in the unit. Lifted my
spirits. Cheap on weekends but
expensive during weekdays
when it's accommodation for
fly-in fly-out workers.

*

Up the street rainbow lorikeets
are taunting a baby possum
stuck high in a tree. Too high
for anyone to do anything.
Unpleasant to witness. The
birds are circling it like sharks –
possum is terrified.

*

On the plane. Already made
a nest of books, notes on the
meeting's agenda, sudokus
and unread photocopied
articles around me. When, in
ten minutes, we know, I'm
going to flick on the inflight
entertainment and watch
whatever comes on for the
next four hours.

Chapter 23
Hearts like dumbbells

October 2017   **Perth and Karratha**

I caught a bus from the airport into Perth and a train out to
Fremantle to attend the strata meeting for the Karratha block
in which we had the two units. *Veep* was on all the way across
to Perth. Great. Tony Hale as Gary Walsh. The flight felt like
half an hour.

> Noon. I'm a wreck. My
> sense of direction – my
> biggest brag – is shot. Was
> completely lost and still
> looking for my hotel when
> I saw I was standing right
> outside it. How it was here
> from its location on the map
> I'll never know. Now having
> a small beer on a couch in
> the pub before a power nap
> when they let me into my
> room and then onto the
> strata meeting.

The day after the meeting, I caught the train back to Perth and then a bus to the airport. Jet-lagged, hot, irritable. The strata meeting was interesting. Hard-working owners trying to get the best deal in a shit situation. The new strata manager and the council of owners worked tirelessly to reduce the insurance premium for the block of units and succeeded. That means a reduction in the strata levies from over $7,000 a year to $4,800 p.a.

Eclectic group. Likeable. Most had lived in Karratha but moved south when the town went bust. They were ordinary in the best sense of the word. Two owners at the meeting had bought their units during the boom for $580,000. A unit in the block was on the market for $55,000. The new owner would have to pay, in addition, a few years of overdue strata levies. The current owner had purchased it for $560,000.

Relaxed train ride. I got the
wrong ticket and everyone
says, 'Don't worry about it –
it's not like they'll throw you off
the train.' So un-Melbourne.

*

Perth airport. Need to haul
myself onto the plane. Had
little sleep. What do I expect
from a $60 room above a
cavernous pub. I had a pub
room once in North Melbourne
that had a busted lock. Maybe
not even a handle. A man
stumbled in, saw me sit bolt
upright in bed, looked around

for what felt like another bed
or a chair, anywhere to drop,
saw nothing and stumbled out.

Karratha

Landed. Nanette picked me up.
Had a mango beer with Bob,
picked up the ute and then
went to the mall to get some
supplies. Motel room. Perfect.
Quiet. Clean. Ground level.
Having an early night.

The temperature was heading towards 38 degrees later in the week. I drove around to see what happened to the houses we sold, and then out to the cemetery to give Dad an update on it all. After that, to Dad's house and then back to the air-conditioned motel room. I wrote a list of what I had to do. I felt dread about the sale of Dad's that I couldn't shake.

I love this motel room.
Spacious. Quiet. Huge bed.
My last day here and then I'm
going to stay in one of Dad's
units.

The motel cleaner came to make up the room. Curved back, few teeth, cross-eyed sweetheart. Late 30s. Her smile lit up her eyes – instantly adorable. I said, 'I'll go out' and she said, 'No, stay, it's so hot outside.' We got talking – I got her story. From Orange in New South Wales. Her husband came to make some money. She asked why I was here. She got my story. We talked so much all she did was make the bed, which is all I had wanted. Someone else to make my bed. We heard her boss outside. She ran into the bathroom. Her boss came by and looked in as she brought the mop out of the bathroom as if she had just finished cleaning it. We smiled. What loveliness. She handed me a bundle of those little shower bottles/soaps. I was almost teary when we parted.

*

The next day I moved across to Dad's unit and the round of meetings began.

*

I stayed the night with E, the droll foreman. I liked him. Welcoming, amusing and easy to be around. Out of nowhere he told me not to fall in love with him. We have a good time. He couldn't care less I was 14 years older – not that he was perhaps aware it was 14 years.

> My behaviour has destroyed
> any illusion that I have class.

I got straight into cleaning up the places. A friend of Dad's and I went through what was left in Dad's house to sort out what was to be kept and what had to go.

I stayed with E again. He called the shots. He was the one who had to get up at dawn and work 12 days straight. The nights were a good temperature. We sat outside at his bamboo Bali bar. More Flintstone than Balinese. He talked a lot, although I saw his shyness. Again, he told me not to fall in love with him. I reassured him I wouldn't. Conceit didn't drive the comment.

Perhaps, for both of us, despite ourselves, we were reminding each other or letting each other see something that we liked or missed.

He had come out of a marriage the previous year. He was still adjusting. He said, as often as he told me not to fall in love, that he 'can't have feelings'.

*

I asked him what he knew about me.

'You're rich.'

He would have heard that at the Rec Club. I wondered if that's why no one in the club, except for Terry, ever bought me a drink and he didn't drink.

*

Even Dad's former accountant hadn't registered the extent of Dad's losses. He told Marcus and me that Dad was worth 4.2 million. When I told him that the estate would be lucky to be worth a seventh of that and then told him what I had to do to get even that. He sat there silent. Ashen.

I was going to put Dad's house on the market. But decided to do it the next day after a clean-up. I was stalling. To sell Dad's house was one of the hardest things I've ever done.

> Met the accountant with my
> parcel of documents. She
> stared at it all. Maybe she was

> surprised to see the pages of
> close-to-unreadable scribbled
> notes from our meeting
> translate into a bundle of 11
> clear and detailed documents.

I drove out to the industrial yard. It looked so different. The shipping containers and dongas were gone. Trucks lined up. Cleared and ordered. Cared for. I loved seeing that.

> My new most loathed word is ...
> plethora
>
> Mine is still 'action' as a verb.
> And always 'journey'.

To see the droll foreman at night was a welcome break from the arduous days. I didn't tell him what was going on during the day. I liked not thinking about it. Again, he told me not to fall in love.

He said I made him feel comfortable. I was relaxed too. He talked a lot about his family back east. Late one night he asked me to count as he called out the names of his first cousins. He remembered 37 out of 45. He said he came from a family of tough men but he was like his dad.

'A lover not a fighter,' he said and looked at me. 'I'm a bit tough.'

He has a ninja tattoo on his chest, another tattoo on his chest that I couldn't make out that he got when he was 16 – his older brother got one at 15 – and a wonky parrot on his arm, drawn by his dad – a version of the parrot on his dad's arm.

We woke at five. He had to go to work. For the week, we had had a running joke about me folding the pile of washing on his spare bed.

'I'm going to put a load on and sweep the kitchen floor ... you've got washing to fold.'

I had told him it was the only domestic chore that I liked. That morning, when he was in the shower, I decided I'd do it. He had been generous all week and it was a thank you gesture. I went like a bullet to get as much folding done as I could. By the time he came into the hallway I had done most of it. I stood back, smiling. He came in and stared at the neat stack of clothes on the bed.

'You folded my washing.'
'Yep,' I said, pretty pleased with myself.

He softened. He looked at me and I saw something cross his face. A new expression. Hard to read. He got dressed and we went outside where he put on his boots. All in silence. We went to our utes. He thanked me for coming over and I thanked him for asking me. Something was up – my folding had unsettled him – but I didn't get it.

I went to the lookout to watch the sunrise and then, after breakfast, back to Dad's to continue the clean-up. His house was not the same without the orb spider. It felt forlorn and devoid of life. All I saw was the lack of love, the disrepair.

> At the cove for a quick swim.
> High tide. 37 degrees, five
> horses with only their heads
> sticking out, their trainers and
> me in the water.

> Marcus sent a text. He wants a
> unit. That's possible. That will
> be fine.

> Stopped on the way back to
> town to watch an iron-ore
> train pass by. Took over five
> minutes. Heading back to the
> unit, via the cemetery, to have
> a shower and then walk into
> the real estate agent. I've
> delayed it for two days. I can't
> delay it anymore.

I didn't hear from E. Shame, as I would have liked to hang out with him. Signing the contract to sell Dad's had made me jangly. I decided to go to the bar at the motel where I had stayed. Only five men at the bar. One was the live-in caretaker of Dad's industrial yard.

'Hello Kev.'
'Oh, it's you ... what have you come to flog this time?'

I bought a drink and joined him. I wanted more of his terseness. I was pleased to hear he had bought his own place in the industrial area. Over the next hour or so, he made quips and frank observations about people I didn't know and a few I did. I loved it.

He came from around northern New South Wales too. Maybe his laconic delivery and direct and straightforward language echoed the language of my childhood. He used words, phrases and expressions that felt deeply familiar. In 2009, I went to the Byron Bay Writers' Festival for work and for three days trailed the sports writer Roy Masters. He was from northern

New South Wales and I couldn't get enough of how he put sentences, observations and stories together.

I remember going back to Dad's unit that night feeling more settled, calmer.

> Driving around today, I
> remembered one thing Dad
> had always wanted – a
> Trevitt St.

Maybe in the early days of the town in the '70s and '80s he could have requested a Trevitt Street but, despite being 'the Prof' at the bar, he would have been too timid to ask.

As I write this, I researched the process but I haven't enough contact with people from Karratha to help make it happen. I need to prove what he gave the community. A 42-year unshakeable love for the town, 35 years of paying rates on multiple properties and putting up tin roofs all over town, and volunteering to put a roof on the Anglican Church's Childcare Centre, I would have thought scored a sign.

'Trevitt St.'
He would never have tired of making detours to drive past it. 'Back up, back up,' he'd say with a big grin and a tight chest, 'Well, lo and behold, what have we got here?'

> Finished doing all I have to
> do. Furnace-hot so hard to get
> going. House and unit emptied
> and cleaned.

On my last night in town the Rec Club had its Oktoberfest. Stalls under tents were set up with different international beers and when I arrived, a cover band was setting up on a small stage in the beer garden.

All the regulars I liked were there. I joined them. N was there. He looked well and not like he had the previous year when he had looked as if he needed to be on a gurney. He told me about the 'good hearts' of two of his friends. One who had big barbeques to feed hungry kids around town and another who saved a dog that had fallen down a well. They were two of the regulars who I looked out for when I went to the club. They always made me feel welcome. They were good men. They understood people need to feel included.

With them was a kooky young bloke in lederhosen or maybe just braces. His mannerisms had an uncanny resemblance to Jacques Tati's character Monsieur Hulot. I wished Dad was there to see him. I showed the young bloke a YouTube clip from *Monsieur Hulot's Holiday*. He was wide-eyed. I wrote down the names of Tati's films. For the rest of the night, every time he passed me, he bent forward, tilting from his ankles, and gave me a high five. If Monsieur Hulot had given high fives, he would have done it in exactly the same lobbing way.

J, the pool player, sat with friends in the beer garden. He avoided my eye and I lacked the courage to approach his table. After an hour or so they got up, as a group, and left.

E hadn't called me since the morning I had folded his washing but, out of nowhere, there he was, sitting at a high table on his own in the beer garden. The night had begun to feel like the final scene of a comedy when all the characters, including the estranged ones, come together at a party or a celebration and everyone makes amends.

He had seen me but pretended he hadn't. I went over to say hello. He asked when I was leaving. I told him tomorrow but he already knew that.

I asked him why he hadn't called. He said, 'You aren't the only person I have to think about.'
After some pressure and asking what was going on, he said, 'I fucking loved being with you. But I can't have feelings, you're going, and then what? What am I supposed to do … I can't have feelings.'

He walked away and I had to walk in the other direction.

I had liked spending time with him too. I liked the connection. Unlike E, I wanted feelings, some shared moments, a tossed-around heart, but having said that, I always had an out. I had a life elsewhere.

At times I feel all of us carry an emotional weight – our hearts like dumbbells a few kilos too heavy to lift.

The last night I had stayed at his house E made a tuna wrap and gave me some. It was piping hot. I said, 'How can you eat that?'
'Because I'm a bit tough.'

We laughed.

He's not tough.

I hope the little ninja on his chest will protect his tender heart.

Last day

What a town.

I'm in a café dressed for a
Melbourne winter yet outside
it's 38 degrees. Fly out in a few
hours for the last time.

*

At the airport, waiting to board.
The strangest thing happened
yesterday.

I was in the cemetery walking around and talking to Dad and the next thing I knew I was in the ute, miles away. It was as if I came to on the highway. I have no recollection of saying goodbye, of leaving the cemetery or of making the decision to head south out of town. Where was I going?

I thought I must have said goodbye, surely, but couldn't for the life of me remember. I thought, I need to go back and then I thought, No. Enough. I've been saying goodbye to Dad all my life. Enough.

*

Recently I found myself watching YouTube videos of American kids whose fathers made surprise visits home from war zones for Christmas. God knows how I ended up there but once there, I was riveted. The reunions made me cry. A lot. The kids were nearly always in classrooms doing ordinary school activities when in walked their fathers. Every time, the kid's initial response was shock and then, moments later, their soft little faces collapsed under the emotion of it all. Every time.

When we were kids, and Dad made his annual trip across from the west to see us, I never crumbled. As I mentioned, we never knew when to expect him to arrive or to leave. He just appeared sometime in our summer holidays. I never let him know how I felt. My heart rushed to him but my body stayed still. Too much emotion. I feared he'd mock me if I ever let him know I missed him more than he must have missed me. Us kids and Dad would stand apart shyly looking at each other. That was how the three of us greeted him and said goodbye to him, for years.

Chapter 24
Always to the wire

October–December 2017   Melbourne and Bowral

In the first week back in Melbourne from Karratha, I saw a friend. She said I looked forlorn. Even a glimpse of intimacy and connection can remind you, or make you see, what you don't have in your life and sometimes that isn't great to see. No one wanted to be reminded that at times they felt lonely.

> Hard not to feel the men
> who fare better in those
> remote towns are the men
> who have women and/or
> families with them.
>
> Sometimes I think men like
> my father should be with a
> woman even if it's the wrong
> woman.

A community-based place like the Rec Club is a haven for men like my father. Three to four hours a day he wasn't alone. Dad's loneliness was more a lostness that he had carried all his life. I felt it even as that little girl who went on pig runs with him, as a primary school kid watching him leave us time and time again and as a young woman in my 20s driving him over Sydney Harbour Bridge to the Mosman Hotel, where he went looking for old friends.

Dad craved connection. I was always happy he had the Rec Club as somewhere to go where he could be with others. A place where he had a stool and a nickname. It meant at times he drank too much – to protect himself, to socialise, to cope, to hide – but, for me, it was more important that my father belonged somewhere.

November

> Yesterday I was taken away from it all.
> Marlon ran the 400m at the All Schools State Carnival and, to our surprise, came second by .08 of a second to the national champ – Jack Peris. Great to watch the boys race to the finish line. All three boys got PBs. Elated kids.
> I had brought three days' worth of food to keep Marlon's energy up but as he said, 'you were the one who chowed down on all of it.'

*

> New short-term tenant in the Karratha unit that my

brother will own soon. First
night, major water pipe bursts
in the upstairs bathroom
wall. Flooded upstairs and
downstairs. Needs plumber,
electrician, carpet-dryer and
possible carpenter.

*

People have gone through
Dad's house. Not interested. All
talked of the work needed.

*

Settlement for the small block
in NSW has come through.

*

Another downpour with
thunder, lightning and hail. Just
put the BBQ away in the nick
of time.
Melbourne.

*

Tomorrow I head down the
highway to Port Arlington – to
a wedding. Only been to a
handful in my life. A friend's
son. Really looking forward
to it as staying overnight.

Maybe I'll hit the road like an
over-eager wedding guest from
a bad comedy to entertain
myself – wet hair in curlers,
five average outfits in the back
of the car to accommodate
any weather changes, orange
streaks on my legs from
a home-tanning job and
pencilled-in clown eyebrows.

*

Pushing through quicksand,
trying to get ready to go to
Port Arlington. Had to make
some calls to Karratha about
the burst water pipe. Fretful.

*

I love my hotel room. I'm
in the 'haunted' upstairs
wall-papered front room
overlooking the bay.

*

My friend, mother of the
groom, gave a speech. Moved
me to tears. Her son's reply
was as heartfelt.

I met my friend around the time she got together with A. Her
son was eight. He was a baby when his father moved back to

England. My friend had seen a lot of step-parent shenanigans and maybe she felt things could have gone either way yet, decades later, here they are – the three of them – and things had worked out.

> Down at the beach. Looks like
> it would be beautiful in the
> water. One soft-bellied bloke
> going in.

*

> I saw a video of mammatus
> clouds. I'd love to see a sky
> packed with those cotton ball
> clouds as much as I want to
> see a murmuration of starlings
> fill a northern sky.

*

> Little interest in Dad's
> place. Potential buyers were
> conscious of the work involved.
> Some liked its size but thought
> it was dated.

At work we all got an email to cancel next week's last class of the year to attend another day of nonsensical PowerPoint presentations. Terrible. Everyone needs a chance to say goodbye. The hard thing coming home from a day of Power-Points is realising you can't recall one point.

> It goes on … in a few weeks we
> have to do a teacher-induction

workshop. Threatened again
with 'You won't be able to work
next year if you don't do it.'
Fifteen years of teaching
experience and a deep love of
the subjects versus a two-hour
workshop. Wish I didn't carry
a fear of the living out of a car
with my kid and dog scenario.

In 2003, when I started work in the TAFE sector, I joined a team of seven or eight teachers. The writing and editing course was vibrant and relevant, the classes were full and had waiting lists. I was green. The co-ordinator had read my short stories in literary magazines and offered me the job. The teachers were good-hearted and generous. They trusted I could do it. They wanted me to succeed. The learning curve was steep. I learnt from trial and error, from books, from students' feedback and from observing and talking to the teachers in my department and in other departments on campus. I also learnt from organised get-togethers with teachers who taught the same course in TAFEs across Melbourne and in regional towns.

Students always came first. There was trust that if something wasn't working or a student was in difficulty, the teachers would work it out together.

Then things changed as auditors and accountants took over and clumps of forms to fill in and boxes to tick began to crowd out our email inboxes. Bureaucracy and compliance kicked in. Corporate language ramped up. Fees were introduced, the chain of managers increased, student numbers dropped and teachers moved on.

By the end of 2017 there were two of us – part-time – and we worked on separate days. Instead of bouncing ideas around with other teachers, you bounced ideas around in your head.

> At Flinders Street station an
> announcement came over
> the speakers wishing us a
> big day shopping.

December

> The moon. Huge and bright.
> Just above the roofs. Looks
> like it's sneaking up on us.

*

> About to accept an offer on
> Dad's house. $165,000. I
> know it's terribly low but it
> needs so much attention and
> every other potential buyer
> has walked away. This buyer
> is from another state.

*

> Had my first seven-hour
> sleep in years. Can't believe
> how I feel.

*

At Casey Fields for an athletics
event for all ages and abilities.
All in athletic gear.
In the grandstand loving the
spectacle in front of me.
Ever seen the *Seinfeld* episode
where Jeff Bridges' father plays
a tough old bloke in Florida
who always wants to take
on Jerry but is no contender.
Similar stuff going on here.
A bloke in his 80s shuffling
down the 100m in a race with
nine-year-old kids. He crosses
the line in just under two
minutes.
Another bloke, maybe mid
60s, ran the 1500 and the 100
before fucking up his knee
in the long jump. He limped
dramatically away to first aid
with the help of two mates,
furious he couldn't run the 400.
He jumped against another old
bloke who jumped one and a
half feet.

*

Mowed the paddock of a
backyard. Always so good to
have the work done.

*

Avoiding the phone as manager
wants to ask me to drop my
hours but still come in two
days a week and teach a
cohort of students who are
extremely demanding. The
unpaid hours, spent outside
the classroom to support some
students over the line, are
more than the hours I get paid.
I have a sty on my eye.

*

Today, instead of marking, I
had a neck/shoulder massage
by a woman called Song who
called me, Sir, and had the
thumbs of a carnival strong
man. Sublime.

*

The settlement for Dad's house
is tomorrow but the transfer
document hasn't arrived
here for me to sign. I have
to wait for the mail and then
get the document signed and
sent back to arrive in Perth
tomorrow ... always to the wire.

*

Tim, my stepfather, turns
80 on Friday. He wants the
extended family in Bowral for
his birthday.

*

I hung around all day waiting
for mail. The document arrived.
I signed it and sent it off so
hopefully the house will sell
tomorrow morning. We leave
tomorrow for NSW for Tim's
birthday.

*

8:30 am. We're boarding from
last gate at end of terminal.
Traffic to airport was heavy.
Outside the terminals was
packed and then once inside
quiet. It's like all of today's
Christmas passengers have
already arrived.

Bowral   New South Wales

Tim had a good birthday. He
looked tired by the end of the
night.

*

Merry Christmas. Marlon is still asleep after a night of watching Rodney Rude videos on YouTube with Justin. Up till 1 am. Rodney Rude is bloody funny. His oversized clown cowboy boots are something else. His belt done up around his knees. And his McDonald's jokes. 'The customer's always fucking McRight.' Oh McGod.

Mcnificent.

Chapter 25
Ol' Whisky

January–June 2018   Melbourne

I had three properties left – a unit in Karratha to sell, another unit to be transferred to Marcus and a timbered block in northern New South Wales to be transferred to Justin. To transfer the Karratha unit, I needed to re-do probate in Western Australia – to show the transfer is fair and in keeping with the requests in Dad's will. A lot of paperwork but thought it shouldn't take too long. Western Australia – I gave it six months.

> A blowfly was in the house.
> The windows were closed
> because it was 40 degrees
> outside. A scorcher. I couldn't
> stand the buzzing and opened
> the window. It flew out. Before
> I could lower the window, it did
> a 360 and flew straight back in.

During this time, people asked if I had been following the Royal Commission into Misconduct in the Banking Industry. Not as much as I would have liked. During one court hearing in the banking royal commission's inquiry, I saw footage of a bank CEO whine that the CEOs shouldn't be personally attacked, and counsel assisting Rowena Orr QC reply, with clarity and measured assertion, that no one was being personally attacked. 'We're just establishing accountability.'

Hard, with Dad in mind, to watch the CEOs go home with millions a year in salaries and bonuses and have the gall to whinge and whine and to shift the blame and wipe their hands clean of any responsibility for their bank's unethical, grubby and, at times, criminal conduct.

> A tenant is leaving a unit –
> hasn't paid rent for the last few
> months. An acquaintance of a
> friend who needed short-term
> accommodation. I rang to say,
> I will be selling, and to give
> him time to find a place and
> frankly pay up. He said, 'I'm
> moving out today.'
> He had been loading his
> belongings into the car while
> we were talking.

My mother called to say Tim was unwell and it's possible he has cancer. Both of them experiencing the awful apprehension of waiting for test results.

> Sleepless night. The tenant
> left so need to organise the
> sale of the last unit and also to
> organise Marlon and my trip to
> the national athletics carnival
> in Sydney.

*

Tim has lung cancer. Mum too
upset to talk so no details but
think it's in his spine too.

*

My eggplant dish. Forgotten.
12 hours in the oven at 160
degrees.

February

Stayed up late to see the
eclipse of the moon. I love
seeing the moon in 3D as it
makes you strangely aware
you are on a planet too.

Bats in the fig tree across the
road went crazy.

*

I went outside yesterday and,
like the blowfly, did a 360 and
came straight back inside.
Stinking hot.

*

Marlon turned 15 last Monday.
Quiet. The night before he was

in a mosh pit at the St Kilda
Festival. Said he felt that was
his party.

*

I needed a new job. So many ludicrous demands. I found it
cynical and upsetting to enrol students without stability or
secure housing and then expect them to have it together
enough to do a demanding full-time Certificate IV course.
Who decided this for them? One student from a job provider
came to class with a luggage trolley of her belongings in two
big suitcases that she never let out of her sight.

Tim is not feeling good. Terrible.

*

I'm at Officeworks trying to
sort out the documents for the
real estate agent for the sale
of the last unit. Need to call
the agent to sort out the forms.
Can't set up a sale without
them.

*

Demands at work never stop
and yet so little time to do the
real work of preparing classes.
We always end up doing that at
home on weekends.

*

One minute I'm told I over-
teach and over-care and the
next I am not making my
teaching hours. What is over-
teaching? Giving a shit?

*

The course is winding up at the
end of this year or next.

*

Working late. I have to look
for a new job. I'm not good at
that stuff. What do I do – walk
around wearing a sandwich
board with a list of my skills
written in poster paint on
the front? I've had so many
jobs yet never had a formal
interview facing a panel asking
me where I see myself in five
years' time. Or to describe a
difficult situation I resolved.
Try selling seven properties in
Karratha in a downturn.

My ideal job would be to set
up a card table in a park and
talk to people like Lucy's
5c Psychiatric Help booth
in *Charlie Brown*. $30 chat
and if they want to nut out
something, I'll listen.

*

New moon. Bats dangling
upside down in the fig tree
over the road.

*

Never really understood the
importance of a holiday without
any pressing work until now.

March

Transfer papers for Justin's
block are on their way to NSW
and the unit in Karratha is on
the market – I feel so much
better when things are moving.

On *Four Corners* I saw banks had given a 71-year-old Western
Australian full-time nurse loans that she couldn't repay. She
had gone to wealth creation seminars. She bought investment properties in the mining boom to secure her future and
then everything went bust and she couldn't rent the places.
Her super went from half a million in 2012 to $540. Now
$3.5 million in debt.

The paperwork in her home office was something to see. She
couldn't move through the room. She needed to surrender
properties to salvage anything but it's all beyond her. You saw,
under the stress, that her cognitive skills and decision-making
capacity weren't up to it.

She's fighting a number of banks as well as dealing with depression. She said the black dog trots behind her. Why weren't they helping her? This will kill her.

She just wanted to be ok in her old age – she's on her own, scared. She made terrible decisions and was encouraged to make them. Conned on all fronts. She said she felt humiliated and she tried hard to do the right thing. She said it's enormously difficult.

Dad.

> On plane to Sydney for
> Marlon's race. We're manning
> the exit door. Marlon joking
> the hostess will call the six of
> us from the exit seats down
> the back for a team huddle.
> Mum is catching a train up to
> see him run. Tim is too unwell.
> I will come back up soon to
> see him.

Sydney

Sydney was so humid. We stayed with friends in Petersham. A suburb I had lived in 30 years earlier when I was in my first year at Sydney University. For the first time since I had left Sydney, in 1993, I felt nostalgia for the place.

> On the train to Olympic Park.
> Streets and streets of redbrick
> flats, white balconies and
> frangipanis.

Marlon's 400m final in 25
minutes. He qualified third. As
the commentator said, This will
be a fast final.

Second, to Jack again.

Thrilling. Put a big grin on
Mum's face. Boy, she needed
it. Two of her friends and her
brother, Sandy, had come to
the race. Sandy lives six hours
away in the country (Quirindi)
so great he came down for the
race and to see Mum.

Melbourne

At baggage carousel. Blockage.
Jammed bags at the opening.
Funny. So tired, everything is
funny.

Had to pull out everything to
not go to bed in my clothes
and sleep beside an unpacked
suitcase.

*

I can hear the Grand Prix at
Albert Park in the background

and at the same time, there's
a huge swarm of insects in
my backyard – incredible
juxtaposition.

*

Woke up, sat up, remembered
not a school day, gave Remy
a pat, fell back onto a pillow,
woke two hours later, sat up,
remembered not a school day,
gave Remy a pat, fell back ...

April

Was out the back tearing up
my back garden. Wish I had a
bulldozer.

Autumn. Nice evening for
ripping things up.

*

No sleep. Left oven on for
13 hours. This time homemade
apple strudel

*

Sitting next to two women on
the tram. One hasn't stopped

talking since they got on. She
can talk under water.

I can text under water.

*

Off to a job interview in
Prahran. One afternoon a
week teaching short narratives
for ten weeks. Won't have
paperwork or boxes to tick as
I'll be a casual teacher.

*

Met the co-ordinator for the
new job. Lovely. Liked each
other straight away. Thoughtful,
imaginative, warm. And sits
at one of the messiest desks
I've ever seen. We showed
each other the photos on our
Work with Children cards and
agreed we weren't photogenic.
In other words, we're sure we
look better in real life. Start
next week.

*

I start the Karratha ring-
around at 11 am – accountant,
valuer and property agent as
soon as they get to work at 9

am. (time difference) And then
onto the Tax Department over
three different things.

*

Saw this as I was driving to
Moorabbin. A van parked on
the side of the road. On a hill.
A tradie was at the back of it
looking for something. It was
out of control in the van. Stuff
jammed in and packed to the
roof. He tugged on a piece of
rope and 15–20 things fell out
onto the road. Some rolled
away. He looked ready to blow.
He picked up two things and
threw them back in and set off
an avalanche. The lights turned
green. The last thing I saw,
as I drove off, was the tradie
throwing his body onto the pile
to try to stop the cascade of
junk falling out.

*

Marlon played footy on Sunday
in a field of white goods hurling
themselves at each other.
Fridges with wispy moustaches.

*

Talked to Tim. Upsetting.
Heading up there soon.

*

Still waiting for valuation on
the unit. Justin's timbered
block is now in his name.

I was paid to prepare classes and teach for seven and a half hours a day. I was still at my desk at 5.45 pm when a call came through on my work phone. A manager rang to tell me that HR had a problem. They said we all were down an hour of teaching a week. She had a solution. The other teacher in my department was going away on annual leave. She suggested I teach the other teacher's two classes of subjects (not my specialities) on Wednesday and her class on Tuesday afternoon for four weeks, to make up the hours.

Unpaid.

I'm not proud of my response.

'Are you fucking, fucking serious?'

Understandably, she didn't appreciate that. After a few heated minutes, we both stopped and I said, 'What are we going to do?'

The manager knew to call me at work, even though I should be home, because, of course, I was still there. That day had been typical. I had spent the day dealing with students' tears, anxieties, stresses – in and out of the classroom, a few email tantrums and one student's struggle with what felt like escalating memory loss. No lunch.

I liked my students. Many of them had things to contend with outside the classroom that played havoc with their capacity to concentrate in class and to complete the assignments. I admired their determination, their courage, to be in the course. I love teaching but when you teach a course with demanding assignments to students coping with difficulties that make study virtually impossible, it calls for more than teaching. I didn't mind this at all. What I did mind, however, was how it went unacknowledged and that no one went in to bat for me. I wanted the best for the students but I was already working long hours and then to be asked to come in and teach new subjects, unpaid, for a month was the last straw.

I'm leaving work. I finish on the first of July.

May

> Footy in Bentleigh. Kids out
> with concussion, broken bones,
> torn hammies and corkies.

> *

> The student who came to class
> with a big smile and her trolley
> of belongings has dropped out.

> I had offered to put her trolley
> in the office and I would guard
> it so she could go out for a
> walk without it.
> She said, 'No.'
> I said, 'I will lock it in the
> office and not be in there.'

She said, 'No.'
I said, 'It's too hard.'
'Very hard,' she said. 'I have to
take everything to the shower
with me.'

*

Thinking about regrets
today. I find it strange when
someone says, 'I have no
regrets.' Or is it something
I just hear being said on
dumb TV shows?

One of my deepest regrets was my response to Dad when he
told his story about shooting Ol' Whisky. During Dad's last
three or four visits, he'd tell the story to anyone who we'd visit
or who visited us. The story always felt it came out of the blue.

When Dad was in his 20s, his parents were going away
for a week. His mother said to him, 'You need to shoot
Ol' Whisky. Your father can't do it. You need to do it
before we get back.'

Ol' Whisky was his father's old red kelpie. A working
dog that, according to my uncle, spent more time under
the house than working. Dad said he thought about it
every day and on the day before his parents came home,
he knew what he had to do. He went over to his parents'
place with his gun. He said he and Ol' Whisky walked
into a paddock. Ol' Whisky had walked ahead. He said
the old dog stopped on a mound, turned around and
looked at him.

'He knew,' said Dad, leaning towards the nearest person listening. 'He knew what I had to do. He looked at me as if to say, "It's ok, John. Go ahead. You have to do it."'

I could never get past the look on Dad's face. I never said a thing. I wish I had said, 'Yeah, you're right, Dad. Ol' Whisky knew you had to do it.'

Posted the final documents
for the settlement of the last
unit – nearly every sale goes
down to the wire.

*

Tim's cancer is in his bones. I
want to sort out a time to visit
him.

*

Spoke to Mum and Tim – They
both sounded so old. The
shock. I said, 'I'm coming next
Friday.' They were pleased.

June

At work, we received an email from a manager about not letting our team down by not getting our 'resultings' in on time. Wasn't a typo – the word appeared twice in the email.

'Resultings.'

I went out the back to see
how my spinach, broccoli and
peas were going. They weren't.
Possums or birds or rats
devoured them all. Every last
bit. And the parsley. For years,
I could grow acres of sweet
parsley.

*

Mum sent a photo of Tim with
a lemongrass room-steamer
beside him, which he loved. In
a text exchange he wrote:

People have been so kind and
thoughtful –
unbelievable.

*

For the first time I can
remember I saw a bloke on
the train move from an aisle
seat into the middle seat so a
woman could sit on the end,
where he had been sitting. I
can't recall a time when I
hadn't had to clamber over or
watch someone else clamber
over a bloke or two, usually on
their phone, to get to a seat.

*

On SkyBus ... still dark.
Smooth run to the airport. Our
landlord visited last night. A
great bloke. Kind. Came to
look at the busted gas heater.
Talks how he writes – few full
stops. Showed us photos of his
daughter's cat and the cat-run
they built, his chooks, his cat
and a fantastic toy musical
merry-go-round he made out
of a microwave.

*

Walked past the captain in
the cockpit. Looks like he's
studying an over-sized folded-
out tourist map.
Sitting in the emergency seat
again. It does remove some of
the panic. Some semblance of
control. This time I'm sitting
next to a poker player playing
with his cards. Beautiful hands.

Card magician, brilliant.

Chapter 26
Goodbyes

June–July 2018   **Bowral and Melbourne**

Tim was very ill but desperate to get his affairs in order. One of the reasons I went up was to join Mum, Tim and a stepbrother in a meeting with the lawyer to talk through the wills. My stepbrother and I were the co-executors of their wills. The wills were complicated as we're a 'blended' family. Mum was struggling in there. She looked stranded and close to tears. She felt the marriage hadn't been acknowledged in earlier meetings. I could see how she felt overlooked. The lawyer didn't look at her or me, instead he directed everything to the men, however, by the end of the meeting, Mum felt better. Reassured. We voiced her concerns and things were being changed so it was clearer where she stood. Tim wanted the best for her and my stepbrother is trustworthy.

Before we left to see the lawyer, Tim had said to me, 'I won't sign my will unless you agree.'

His will. I was so moved.

> I went for a walk thinking
> about Mum. Dead set, how can

you let someone leave your
office feeling bamboozled over
their own will.

*

I'll go up again soon.

Melbourne

After work – teaching in a nearby suburb – I would walk
home. Long walks cutting through back streets and laneways.
I needed to. Another delay. Settlement of the last unit had hit
a snag – something to do with the financial lending contract to
the new owner.

*

I must have been stressed. I was photocopying notes for
students in my new workplace and I don't know how it
came about but the next thing I knew I was blurting out to
the impossibly handsome young man at the administration
desk that I was a Jacks champion. He looked perplexed,
maybe bemused, but that didn't stop me going on to tell him
I used real sheep knuckles and how as an adult I challenged
Victoria's Jacks champion. I represented New South Wales.
Probably only told him because I won. (For the record, we
gave ourselves the title of state champion as neither of us had
ever been beaten. The game could have gone either way. We
were each other's toughest opponent.) I walked away thinking
what the fuck just happened. Still, now he'll know, if or when
he sees me again, I'm Australia's undefeated Jacks champion.

*

I handed the rest of the transfer of Marcus's unit to the settlement agent. I couldn't face it. It won't be done by the end
of the financial year, which meant I couldn't wrap it all up. I
should have done it but I couldn't face any more bureaucracy.

*

Tim's will came through attached to an email – 37 pages.
Blended families. He tried so hard to get everything sorted and
tied up. The lawyer was worried about wills being contested
or one side of the family getting 'it all'.

I wanted this to be resolved quickly for Tim's sake. We all did.
Everyone involved saw he was growing weaker by the day.

> I'm folding washing in front of
> the heater and a footy game.
> Meditative. One of my favourite
> things about winter.

*

> Dad's final unit is still not
> settled. The financial bloke who
> made the mistake has been
> uncontactable. Meanwhile the
> costs of leaving the unit empty
> continue.

*

Today three people are being
interviewed for my job, in an
office off the open-plan office
where my desk is, while I'm
here.

How 'resulting'.

Thank God the students
appreciate me. I told them I
won't be back next semester.
They have been great. Two or
three are shaken. They know
how hard we have worked
together to get them over
the line.

During that week, I talked to an experienced community nurse
who provided home health care for people in dire straits. We
talked about the bureaucratic hell she dealt with. She said the
nurses used to work together as a team and they were always
effective and efficient. They trusted each other and things ran
smoothly. They had freedom to find innovative ways to help
but now she's answerable for decisions made by inexperienced
operators in a call centre about someone's care. No continuity.
No consistency. She blamed HR.

The historian Donald Horne said back in the 1960s that Australia is a lucky country run by second-rate bureaucrats.

The nurse is from northern
NSW too. She described a
painting featured in a public
place that I would almost
travel the two days to see. A

woman is mounting a horse.
Her right foot is in the stirrup
and if you follow the line of
action she's about to make,
she'll be up on the horse in the
saddle, backwards.

How can this growing bureaucracy, compliance and distrust
and as another TAFE teacher said, 'The outrageously unrea-
sonable things you are asked to do for the sake of job security',
not be linked to banks and an anxiety around debt?

I must be at a low ebb –
haven't folded any washing
all week. The pile looks as
unappealing as the dishes in
the sink.

I wanted to get all the TAFE work completed as soon as possible. I wanted to visit Tim. Things weren't good with him. This
involved a lot of extra work to encourage students to get their
assignments in. I couldn't stand for some of them to give up
so close to the end and reinforce an already trampled sense
of self.

One more class, ten more
assignments to mark, record
the 'resultings' and it's over.
Just have to clear the desk. A
student called in. The hardest
working student yet whose
memory is slipping by the day.
Don't know why. He's not going
to get through. Snaps your
heart in two.

I started clearing my work desk
and will go in on Saturday to
more or less finish it when no
one is there. It feels good.

I want to clear it out and get
out before anyone notices I
have gone.

Late June

Marlon's doing work experience
with a carpenter. Two
apprentices. One is a 'legend.'
The apprentices are obsessed
with Tinder. They have Tinder
Premium, whatever that
means. They spend smoko
swiping on Tinder. One said
to the other, 'Soon it won't be
called, "Smoko". It'll be called
"Swipo".'

I don't get online dating.

You need a thick skin to do online dating. Tough. I mean who
can bear the idea of strangers swiping their hands across your
face. And surely profiles stray from the truth. They aren't
going to write – I live like a fox. I sulk for attention. I have a
surprising lack of curiosity about anybody. I bushwalk in the
hope of finding a place to dig a shallow grave.

I'm not tough enough. I'm not one of those people who
can extract myself easily from a set-up situation. I know

quickly – minutes – whether I want to hang around or not. I swell with panic if someone's expectations don't match mine. If they want more, I can't assert myself and leave. Instead, I feel guilty that I want to go so I stay and give mixed messages. I make things messy. I create misunderstandings. I've never understood how to deal with the expectations of dating.

> In the city finalising things.
> Packed up my desk. Loaded up
> my suitcase with my reference
> books and folders.

*

> Tim is almost bedridden.
>
> I'll head up the end of the
> week. Mum is exhausted.

July

> Went to photocopy my last
> piece of information for a new
> teacher and my photocopying
> card fell broken to the floor. I
> loved that piece of plastic.
>
> In ten minutes, there will be
> no trace of me … as if I were
> never here.
>
> Can't get the smile off my face.

*

I better get up. I have a job to
leave.

Handover day. It hurt to hand over that broken photocopy
card and know it will never be replaced. I should have a life-
time membership to that machine. I had completed all that
I needed to do in my own time but was expected to come in
for two more days and what, fill in another pile of auditing
forms for the next semester? I wasn't going to do that. I was
a wreck. I needed to see Tim. I was told I had to get a medical
certificate as having two consecutive non-teaching days off.
Fifteen years in the job and I had never had a sick day or had a
teaching day off except for when someone close had died.

At doctor's waiting with my
bag of folders. I flicked open a
magazine to see a full-page ad
with Elizabeth Taylor in a white
one-piece kneeling on sand
and looking exquisite. Beside
her is her quote: 'Pour yourself
a drink, put on some lipstick
and pull yourself together.'

Home. Let the cull begin. I
walked in the door, put my
bag down and started on the
bathroom.

Next day

10:47 pm – just stopped
cleaning. Finished the
bathroom, my bedroom and

the living room and hallway.
Kitchen tomorrow. Work room
Saturday. I can't celebrate the
end of work until it's done. The
state of my place just reminds
me of the countless hours of
unpaid work I'll never get back.

*

Cleaned, around the clock, for
four days. Sparkling.

*

I'm watching *The Office* and
doing paperwork for the
estate's final tax. I'm shuffling
paper, loathing it, as I watch
Michael try to set up his own
paper company.

*

Picked the olives from the tree
in the backyard. If I can sell
seven properties in a mining
bust, I can make brine.

*

I'm walking to the post office
to post a parcel of paperwork
to the Karratha accountant
for the last return for the

estate. She'll call me to ask
for something but it will be
manageable. It's done. Soon it
will be over.

*

Waiting in the airport for the
plane to NSW to see Tim.
Watched a dad take a selfie
with his two little daughters.
Selfies are usually shit photos.
I offered to take some. One
of my favourite things to do –
take photos of people in this
situation. I'll cross the street to
offer – especially if I can see
that someone from the group
will miss being in the shot.
Never been refused.
Good ones of the dad despite
his missing front tooth. Loves
his kids.

Bowral

Mum met me in tears at Bowral train station. Tim was completely bedridden – unable to adjust himself in his bed. Mum was spinning. Tim's daughter, Fiona, had come across from western New South Wales to nurse him.

Tim was so weak. One day I thought was his last but the next day, he rallied and said he felt a bit better. Mum, my step-siblings and I gathered around his bed to talk about the memorial service. He said he would love me to write a eulogy. I cried. The request showed he knew I loved him.

> God, it's sad. Mum is breaking
> down a lot – grief and
> exhaustion.

> My family are criers. If anyone in
> my family cries, I cry.

I had to say goodbye to Tim. I kept walking past his room crying and not wanting to go in. Finally, I walked in. Mum was in there. I told him I loved him and he said, 'I love you too, sweetheart.'

We hugged and I had to go.

Melbourne

> Home. Wretched after a
> sleepless night in a sleeper.
> Fantastic companion. Pauline
> from Geelong. A droll primary
> school teacher. A rare gift.
> One of the true, old-school
> teachers – unconventional,
> imaginative, practical, kind,
> straight-up and generous. Her
> students and their parents
> would never forget her.

> Her father worked on the
> railways. She spent a lot of her
> childhood on trains and now,

during school holidays, she
travels on trains up and down
the east coast.

I can see how being on a night
train and watching the inky
landscape fly past and hearing
the muted sound of bells ring
out at level crossings could
lull you as an adult if that was
a part of your childhood. Like
rain on a tin roof.

On the morning of July the 25th, Tim died. At home. Mum and
his three children were with him.

Chapter 27
Hit the ball with love

July–August 2018   **Bowral and Melbourne**

Tim came into our lives in the '70s. The early years of a blended family was a time of adjustment for all of us but, looking back, I saw Tim wanted everything to be ok. He wanted everything to work out and be harmonious. However, at times, negotiating the needs of eight people was beyond him, beyond all of us. Especially when all eight were jammed into a car on a long hot car trip with one kid sitting on the console blocking the air-con from reaching the five of us along the backseat.

Tim kept things close to his chest but he must have found it puzzling to have six teenagers of a new generation, who, when leaving school or university, wanted freedom and not to race into full-time employment, especially in an office. Tim loved an office, both at home and at work. Unlike Dad, he left rows and rows of neatly stacked labelled boxes of files full of meticulously ordered numbers, columns and calculations.

Everyone knew they could trust Tim and rely on him, including Dad. That must have made it easier for Dad to drive the 5,000 kilometres back to Karratha each year.

Tim always did the right thing by me. His responses were consistent and measured. He listened well. He never let a disagreement get in the way of the relationship.

Fiona nursed her dad in his last month. She is not a trained nurse so it's one thing to want to be able to nurse someone who is dying and another, to do it. And another, to do it beautifully. When I said goodbye to Tim, I said, 'You are in good hands', and he said, 'I know. It's remarkable.'

He surrendered to her care. He trusted she knew his needs. Fiona made it possible for Tim to die at home where he wanted to be.

> At the end of the memorial service, Justin said to me, 'That was as good as any Lassie movie.'

> *

> Marcus is here. He had been here for a few days. He's been a fantastic support for Mum. He's reconnected with Mum's old friends who adore him.

> He said to one friend, 'Margaret, before you go, I've got a golfing tip.' (Earlier they had talked golf.) He pretended to swing at a ball.

'Forget your shoulder and your
left hand,' he said. 'Hit the ball
with love.'

*

Hard to leave Mum. Really
hard. She's coming down to
stay with us soon.

August

Melbourne

Teaching novel writing to
Diploma students. I told the
students that I was sorry I
had missed the class last week
but my stepfather had died. A
student stopped what she was
doing and asked if I was all
right.
I lost composure for a few
moments. And for the next few
minutes, we sat in silence as I
held back tears and collected
myself. New class. New
students. I like them.

Too much too soon.

Her kindness showed me that.

Fiona said when Tim died that she felt it at a cellular level. I didn't feel that when Dad died. The sheer workload of being the executor of his estate left little time or space to mourn his death but that's not why. The truth was I felt the loss at that level the first time he left us. This time around was easier.

I felt an ache in my chest one afternoon in the psychiatrist's room where I was eight again, crying in my grandmother's car as she drove my brothers and me out of Uralla and I watched everything I knew and wanted disappear.

> I read a quote from a US film reviewer how happiness and pain aren't found in big ideas but in the little victories and defeats of childhood.

I often think of an early evening in Karratha when I stood on the edge of Dad's front yard waiting to show my brother a scene. We were cleaning up for the sale of his house. The air had cooled but was still warm. Dad's gum trees cast long shadows over the house and a pink evening haze had settled over the streets of Bulgarra. Marcus was pulling out a misshapen shrub beside the house and, across the road, Aboriginal kids ran around in a gully of ghost gums and shopping trolleys.

I heard 'Greensleeves' before I saw the ice-cream van in a street behind the gully. I wanted to show my brother the contrast between the electric-wild kids and the Mr Whippy van going up and down the streets as slow as a hearse.

*

The last transfer of Dad's properties came through on the night of my stepfather's memorial service. Marcus owns his piece of Karratha.

Seven months later, in 2019, on the night of the third anniversary of Dad's death, the estate's final tax bill came through. I paid the bill that night. It was over.

*

Dad was, and is, often in my thoughts. Whenever I sit down to write a short story, I don't know what I will write about. The characters are always made up however once a story emerges, I always see links back to my small-town upbringing and to him. Dad saw this too. He had read all my stories. He said he kept them next to his bed.

Once on the phone, Dad asked, 'What are you doing this afternoon?'
I said, 'Writing a story.'
'What about?'
'Don't know,' I said.
'Well, don't write about your ol' man.'

Yeah, righto, Dad.

Acknowledgements

I would like to thank my long-term editors, Alistair Stewart and Kathleen Mary Fallon, who have been with me since I started writing short stories.

Alistair knew my father and the situation well. He supported me throughout those years and worked with me to pull all the material together.

Kathleen, my mentor and friend, recognised I had something to say and gave me the courage to write it. Her brilliance always at hand.

Thank you to my readers, Amanda Roe, Michael Epis, Oliver Cocks, Pascale Baelde, Jennine Primmer and my dear friend, the late Madeleine Preston, for their invaluable comments.

Thank you to Andrea McNamara for helping me start the process of getting it out and to Jocelyn Hungerford for her thoughtful and final editing sweep.

I appreciate my family – my mother, my brothers and my sister – for their humour and generosity in allowing me to write freely about Dad and the difficult times in our shared history. When I asked Justin if anything needs to be changed, he said, 'bulldozer is one word.'

Thank you to my son, Marlon. He lived through all of it with me and never once complained.

I'd like to thank my friends for their patience and understanding and for letting me have a friendship through text messages over those two and a half years of sorting out the mess.

Thank you to my neighbour David Layton for opening up his home office with as little notice as it takes to cross a road. And thank you to Stephanie Crolla, Mum and Alistair Stewart for making the trips over west possible.

To Terri-ann White, what can I say?
Little can match the thrill of going to my inbox and opening Terri-ann's late-night email to say, having just finished my manuscript, that she'd love to take it on for Upswell. Many, many thanks.

About Upswell

Upswell Publishing was established in
2021 by Terri-ann White as a not-for-profit
press. A perceived gap in the market for
distinctive literary works in fiction, poetry
and narrative non-fiction was the motivation.
In her years as a bookseller, writer and then
publisher, Terri-ann has maintained a watch
on literary books and the way they insinuate
themselves into a cultural space and are
then located within our literary and cultural
inheritance. She is interested in making books
to last: books with the potential to still be
noticed, and noted, after decades and thus
be ripe to influence new literary histories.

About this typeface

Book designer Becky Chilcott chose
Foundry Origin not only as a strong,
carefully considered, and dependable
typeface, but also to honour her late
friend and mentor, type designer Freda
Sack, who oversaw the project. Designed
by Freda's long-standing colleague,
Stuart de Rozario, much like Upswell
Publishing, Foundry Origin was created
out of the desire to say something new.

www.ingramcontent.com/pod-product-compliance
Lightning Source LLC
Chambersburg PA
CBHW031043110426
42740CB00048B/800